PRIMAL TEAMS

Primal Teams

Harnessing the Power of Emotions to Fuel Extraordinary Performance

JACKIE BARRETTA

⊿AMACOM

AMERICAN MANAGEMENT ASSOCIATION

New York • Atlanta • Brussels • Chicago • Mexico City • San Francisco
Shanghai • Tokyo • Toronto • Washington, D.C.

Bulk discounts available. For details visit:
www.amacombooks.org/go/specialsales
Or contact special sales:
Phone: 800-250-5308
Email: specialsls@amanet.org
View all the AMACOM titles at: www.amacombooks.org
American Management Association: www.amanet.org

This publication is designed to provide accurate and authoritative information in regard to the subject matter covered. It is sold with the understanding that the publisher is not engaged in rendering legal, accounting, or other professional service. If legal advice or other expert assistance is required, the services of a competent professional person should be sought.

Library of Congress Cataloging-in-Publication Data
Barretta, Jackie.
    Primal teams : harnessing the power of emotions to fuel extraordinary performance /
Jackie Barretta.
        pages cm
    Includes bibliographical references and index.
    ISBN-13: 978-0-8144-3441-3 (hardcover)
    ISBN-10: 0-8144-3441-X (hardcover)
    ISBN-13: 978-0-8144-3442-0 (ebook)
    ISBN-10: 0-8144-3442-8 (ebook)
    1. Teams in the workplace. 2. Employee motivation. 3. Psychology, Industrial.
4. Organizational behavior. I. Title.
    HD66.B373 2015
    658.4'022—dc23   2014014380

About AMA
American Management Association (www.amanet.org) is a world leader in talent development, advancing the skills of individuals to drive business success. Our mission is to support the goals of individuals and organizations through a complete range of products and services, including classroom and virtual seminars, webcasts, webinars, podcasts, conferences, corporate and government solutions, business books and research. AMA's approach to improving performance combines experiential learning—learning through doing—with opportunities for ongoing professional growth at every step of one's career journey.

Printing number
10 9 8 7 6 5 4 3 2 1

CONTENTS

ACKNOWLEDGMENTS

I've known for a long time that I would write a book about teams that included scientific concepts you just don't see in the typical business book. My many years as a leader in various companies convinced me that we need to learn so much more about the incredible power of group dynamics, but I've found it difficult to express on the page what many neuroscientists and I have begun to understand about unleashing that power.

Gradually, however, I found the words as I have shared my ideas with thousands of people during public presentations, corporate training, and consulting. I owe you all a great debt of gratitude. Readers of my blog deserve special mention for giving me honest feedback and tremendous encouragement. Thank you, each and every one, for listening to me, challenging me, and enlarging my understanding. I most deeply appreciate the faithful and unrelenting advice of Jeffrey Barnes, Steve Bell, Manoj Garg, Greg Sievers, and my father, Tony.

My agent and collaborator Michael Snell has served as my #1 listener and shaper. He asked penetrating questions to help me hone the message, suggested many of the right words to capture concepts and bring them to life, and told me in no uncertain terms when he thought I had gone too far or fallen too short in my musings. No author could wish for a better teammate. Thanks, Michael, for all your support and good humor.

I must also thank my editor at AMACOM Books, Bob Nirkind, who read every word of the manuscript as it flowed from my word processor. His thoughtful editing constantly pushed me to think more deeply about what I wanted to say and to make sure I dotted every "i" and crossed every "t."

All of the teammates with whom I've worked, all of the teams I have led, and all of the teams leaders who have guided me over the past few decades have contributed to this as well. I feel such abiding appreciation for all of the learning experiences we have shared.

Finally, thank you to my husband, Jim; my many family members, especially my mother Marian; and my many dear friends who have kept life fun and fulfilling through all of the sacrifices an author must make as she struggles to commit a lifetime of experience to the page.

PRIMAL TEAMS

"Since Feeling Is First …"

I borrowed the title of my Prologue from an e. e. cummings love poem because it so nicely captures the reason I wrote this book. Why would I start a business book with a line from a love poem? Because love is one of our most powerful primal feelings. And primal feelings fuel the brainpower that drives the best team performances.

This book was born out of feelings, painful feelings. Not long ago, my life took a sharp turn when I lost something that I dearly cherished. I had been leading a large IT group for over a decade, one with a unique vitality that fostered great success and deep satisfaction, but the team's energy was waning. Our CEO had just retired, our company was merging with another company, and we could feel our once exceptional and vibrant culture, with its focus on the sanctity of teams, giving way to a more conventional and moribund one.

Years before, we had hit on a winning formula for what we called high-performance teams. One tenet of that formula placed a huge priority on giving a strong voice about running the organization to the teams who played such a major role in getting results. Team members loved that responsibility and responded with great enthusiasm. We paid a lot of attention to how people felt about their work, their emotional relationships to the organization, and their feelings for one another. In that environment, people performed masterfully. Even our customers and competitors could see something special in "the way we do things around here." Now, as the merger took effect, a lot of the optimal emotions that had driven our success began to seep away. I left the company and founded the Nura Group, a consulting and training company that specializes in helping individuals and teams improve their ability to create game-changing innovations. Although the flame that inspired innovation at my former employer had faded away, my passion for what we had built had kept burning. Could I pass the torch to others?

That question led to many others. Could I define and describe the energy that drove us to achieve so much? Why did it make such a difference to our creativity and performance? Could I teach it to others? To answer those questions, I began a quest that included immersion in the latest developments in psychology, neuroscience, and even quantum physics. I poured through spiritual texts for inspiration and insight. I took a master's degree in organizational development. I searched my heart and wracked my brain. In the end, my heart won.

Along my journey, I learned a lot about our primal human nature and how optimal emotions naturally evoke the most sought-after contemporary team competencies, from quickness, flexibility, and resilience to innovation and complexity management. Back at my old job, we never really talked about emotion, preferring, as most businesspeople do, to toss around terms like "empowerment" and "engagement" and "motivation" and "innovation." But as I learned more and more about what separates good teams from great teams, I came to understand that superperformance depends on creating a work environment that respects and taps into the power of what Mother Nature has hardwired into our brains, the power of our emotions.

I've worked with a lot of clients since I began developing the idea of primal teams, and I've taken great satisfaction from seeing the practices I teach actually transform teams as they learn to *harness the power of emotions to fuel extraordinary performance.* The results speak for themselves.

Gradually, I have built a vocabulary to describe an experience that can feel like pure magic but often defies words. I have tried very hard to find the right words so that I can share what I've learned with my readers, that is, all the team leaders and team players who want to feel the thrill of doing their best work in the best possible environment. That brings me back to the word "love," but not with its conventional connotation of wide-eyed, gushy sentiment but rather in the sense of a basic and powerful human emotion that can conquer fear and ignite vitality. Love uniquely facilitates optimal cognitive function, enhanced perception, heightened inspiration, and crystal-clear insight.

Rational thinking, logic, and mathematical models will always play a role in solving our most challenging business problems, but they're never as sharp as when powered by the beating human heart. That's where the energy starts, with our emotions. Only by working directly with our emotions can we release the energy we need to become world-class creative problem solvers.

Many other authors have written fine books about team performance and employee engagement and emotional intelligence. I've read most of them and have found their observations quite useful. However, I have chosen not to repeat their excellent advice in this book but instead to explore many of the latest, most eye-opening, and often quite unconventional ideas and techniques that put more heart into the performance equation. With these tools, anyone who leads or works on a team can harness the optimal emotions that fuel the highest levels of success and satisfaction—and help teammates do the same.

I'll close by paraphrasing my favorite line from the e. e. cummings poem:

"the best gesture of my brain is less without my heartbeat's power"

—Jackie Barretta

CHAPTER 1

Hidden Energy

Unleashing Maximum Potential

Over a decade ago, IBM met a challenge that would have destroyed most businesses. IBM's leaders, recognizing that the company could not sustain a viable future relying on the hardware that had made it a household name, initiated a complete transformation of the company from a hardware manufacturer to a global problem solver. Their new business model deployed smart teams to work creatively with clients on the development of customized solutions to complex business problems. Instead of just selling PCs to a customer, IBM now fields teams who analyze the customer's workflow to determine the functions that equipment, such as mobile devices, could enable employees to perform optimally.

Transforming the company from building one-size-fits-all products to developing one-of-a-kind solutions to meet unique needs took courage. Such a huge and risky strategy would capsize most companies, but IBM isn't most companies. Its employees often say they "bleed blue," meaning the IBM spirit and culture run through their veins. Their deep emotional connection to the company helped motivate them to persevere through a difficult transition and played a key role in their success as members of smart, creative teams. The emotional connections and sensations that people feel in the workplace can empower them to come up with innovative solutions to their clients' most challenging problems. At IBM, emotions—as much as, if not more than, IQ or any other measure of brilliance—stimulated people to make their new service business succeed in a radically altered marketplace.

In this chapter, you'll discover that your organization already contains a treasure trove of similar problem-solving potential that you're able to release by stirring optimal (i.e., distinctly upbeat and deeply felt) emotions in your people.

SPARKING THE CREATIVE BRAIN

I vividly recall the magic that happened one day in a software development team I was leading. The CEO of our company, a trucking giant, had challenged us to alter our computer systems to support a new railroad service he wanted to launch in four weeks. We felt highly motivated and had spent every waking moment over a two-day period straining to find a quick way to modify our trucking software to work for railroads. Sitting together in a conference room, batting around ideas, and drawing diagrams on the whiteboard long after the other company's teams had gone home for the day, one of our teammates, Jake,[1] voiced our basic fear: "We just can't do it in four weeks. These changes are going to take at least four *months*."

Although I respected Jake, I felt we could do better. "Let's shift our emotions," I suggested. Several heads nodded agreement. We all needed a break from fear and anxiety. "Forget about all these alternatives and diagrams," I continued. "Let's take the problem and put it on a mental shelf alongside our anxiety." I then led an exercise (which I'll outline later in this chapter) to get everyone de-stressed, centered, and feeling positive. Once the energy in the room had shifted, I said, "Now let's pull the problem off the shelf, leave all the anxiety behind, and see what happens." It took only a few minutes before Jake exclaimed, "I've got it! I know how we can solve this quickly." He had devised an elegant solution we could implement in a scant few weeks.

Make Creativity Job One

The success of an organization depends on those key moments when teams develop creative ways to provide greater value to customers and perform more efficiently in increasingly demanding situations. Too often, a team under pressure falls prey to negative emotions like fear and anxiety and formulates an unimaginative solution that barely gets the job done, takes an eternity to implement, and requires constant re-pair. However, when they replace fear and anxiety with optimal emo-tions such as joy and playfulness, they find it a lot easier to dream up solutions that delight customers, rapidly deliver value, and elegantly evolve along with the business.

A 2010 IBM survey reported that the majority of over 1,600 global CEOs agree that the success of their companies rests on the creative problem-solving capabilities of their people. That's the only way their companies can handle the accelerating complexity of today's business terrain, with all of its disruptive technological innovations, quickly evolving customer expectations, constantly shifting government regu-lations, dramatic swings in the global economy, and overwhelming vol-umes of data.

You must instill creativity at every level, from the senior executive team to the help desk staff, because you cannot afford to waste valuable time waiting for decisions to travel up and down the food chain. By then, impatient customers will have switched to your competition. While executives in the IBM survey agreed that organizations should encourage creativity in frontline workers, they admitted that they did not know how to do that.[2]

Whether your team must solve an internal design problem or invent the next disruptive breakthrough in your industry, they won't exceed your expectations unless you make it clear that creativity is Job One and develop an environment that fosters innovative thinking. Don't leave creativity to chance; shape it by design. Most businesses today focus intently on enabling data-based decisions and streamlining their processes, but these tactics will never spark the creativity needed to get and stay ahead of the competition. Creativity and innovation require the right state of mind. Fortunately, new research in psychology and neuroscience suggests that you can employ specific methods to put any team in the state of mind where creativity becomes a habit.

Design for Creativity

Creative thinkers see reality in new and exciting ways. Most people looked at a cell phone and saw a small screen useful only for displaying data, but to Steve Jobs it looked like an opportunity to *input* data as well. His insight led to the iPhone's touch screen features. Our teammate Jake solved the railroad problem by thinking differently about our existing software, leading him to the idea of combining database elements in an atypical way that "fooled" our existing trucking system into processing railway routes just as accurately. Our talented team had racked their brains for two days, yet the answer finally came in a flash of insight when they began experiencing optimal emotions.

It takes time and effort, but you really can encourage and develop a team's knack for creative thinking and problem solving. Take the classic so-called candle task problem. This exercise, often used in creativity research, involves giving someone a box of tacks, a candle, and a book of matches. They're asked to attach the candle to a wall (or a corkboard) in such a way that it will burn without dripping wax onto the floor. You have 10 minutes to solve the problem. What would you do?

A creative thinker would empty the tack box, then tack the box to the wall as a candleholder. Now the candle will not drip wax onto the carpet. The solution hinges on seeing the tack box not just as a storage unit for tacks but also as a potential candleholder. People naturally link the tacks and the box so closely in their minds that they can't easily separate them to solve the problem. How can you get team members to (pardon the cliché) think outside the box? What causes a person to think of using the box in a novel way, and how do you intentionally spark this ability in a person or team?

In 1987, American psychologist Alice Isen conducted experiments that tested the effect of emotion on subjects' ability to solve the candle task. After dividing them into four groups, she induced a particular emotional mood in each. She put the first group into a positive mood by showing them five minutes of funny television bloopers. She soured the mood of the second group by screening five minutes of a documentary film showing Nazi concentration camps. She then dampened the emotions of the third group by presenting a five-minute segment of a math film illustrating the method for calculating area under a curve. The final control group received no emotional manipulation. After the groups had viewed the films, and before they had begun the candle task, Dr. Isen questioned them to ensure that they did feel the intended emotions.

The results of these experiments clearly demonstrated the impact of emotions on problem solving. The subjects in the group experiencing positive emotions were three times more likely to find the solution than the other groups. Isen found little difference among the three other groups.[3]

In 2008, Carsten De Dreu, Matthijs Baas, and Bernard Nijstad published an article in the *Journal of Personality and Social Psychology* that provided an extensive review of research on the impact of emotions on creativity, including an account of the authors' own comprehensive original research in which they measured the impact of mood on subjects' creative fluency and originality while performing brainstorming tasks. The scientists discovered that emotions play a major role in our ability to see the world differently. Our emotions can either open up our minds to see new possibilities, or they can close down our minds in a way that keeps the same old thoughts swirling around in our brains. So which emotional states make us better creative problem solvers?

Apply Positivity and Arousal

According to the article by De Dreu, Baas, and Nijstad, optimal team emotions that spark creativity begin with positivity. When people experience positive emotions, they gain an expanded perspective that enables them to relate to and integrate divergent material innovatively. Emotions such as cheerfulness and optimism make people feel less constrained and more apt to take risks and explore novel solutions to problems. They also prompt the inclusive thinking that opens people's minds to uncommon perspectives. That's when you decouple the tacks from the box or your existing software from truck routes.

Researchers who conducted one study cited in the article asked participants in positive moods to rate how well a particular object fit within a specified category. They found that these individuals tended to include atypical items in a category. For example, they would more likely include an elevator, a camel, and feet in a category labeled "vehicle" than would a control group of people experiencing a wide range of moods. Good moods open our minds to new possibilities.

On the other hand, negative emotions, such as anger and frustration, signal to individuals that their situation is problematic and that they must take constrained, analytical action to remedy it. Negative emotions shut down their openness to novel possibilities.

Positive emotions come in different sizes, ranging from a low level of arousal to extreme passion. The research article by DeDreu, Baas, and Nijstad provides a thorough examination of the impact of emotional arousal on creativity. As in the "Three Bears," Baby Bear emotions may be too small, Papa Bear emotions too big, but Mama Bear emotions are just right. Low levels of arousal, such as contentment, promote inactivity, whereas extremely high levels of arousal, such as excitement, reduce our capacity to perceive and evaluate information. It's difficult to think clearly when our extreme passion creates a state of exhilaration or euphoria. At moderate levels of arousal, people feel optimally motivated to seek and consider multiple alternatives. Moderate levels of arousal also enhance working memory, which in turn enhances cognitive flexibility, abstract thinking, and access to long-term memory.[4]

Primal team leaders take specific steps to help people experience the appropriate levels of arousal and the optimal level of positive emotions because they know that such a state releases the utmost creativity. They pay close attention to the emotions running through their team, and, whenever necessary, they take sure steps to reshape less than optimal emotions. While they can't force an individual or team to think creatively, they can help them open the door for creativity.

Optimal emotions also help teams meet the other challenges teams face in today's high-pressure workplace, including mind-boggling complexity, nerve-wracking changes that require impossibly agile responses, and other unpredictable disruptive events that can send a team into a tailspin.

DEEPENING THE IMPACT

Several years ago, Subaru launched a "Love" advertising campaign that highlighted the emotion that drivers feel for their Subarus. In a *Washington Times* article, columnist Marybeth Hicks berated the company for citing love as a reason for buying a car. Hicks argued that an irrational emotion like love should not influence rational purchasing decisions or any other business deliberations.[5] Although most business leaders would probably agree with Hicks, according to new research into the connection between the heart and the brain, Subaru was on to something.

Positive, moderately aroused emotion may stimulate our brain to function more creatively, but heartfelt emotion boosts our creative ability to an even higher level. Our heart has a unique ability to put us in our most creative state.

Pull the Strings of Heartfelt Emotion

What exactly do we mean by "heartfelt" emotion? How does it differ from positive emotion? Does it deserve any role in a business environment? The answer is a resounding yes. Let's see why. Simply put, positive emotions include pleasant thoughts and calm sensations in our body, whereas heartfelt emotions consume our attention and activate a strong sensation in the actual area of our heart. You know the feeling. Think about someone you love "with all your heart." When you picture that loved one in your mind, don't you feel a warm, tingling sensation in the area of your heart? Most people do.

In a team, the two types of emotion play out differently:

Positive Emotion	Heartfelt Emotion
Relief when a project is finished	Boundless delight when a completed project delivers great value to the organization
Satisfaction with a bonus or big raise	Unbridled appreciation for a supportive boss
Thankfulness when a teammate works overtime to complete a crucial task	Tremendous gratitude for your teammate's efforts and sacrifices

Note that the list on the left suggests relatively mild feelings, whereas the one on the right embodies deeper feelings that border on love. "I *love* making our customers happy!" I *love* the way my boss supports my work!" I *love* it when Rick throws himself into the work." Strong heartfelt emotions can halt our rational mental processes and connect us to people in a much more profound way than relatively mild feelings, such as relief or satisfaction or thankfulness. Heartfelt emotions make our hearts sing, and they set fire to our cognitive and perceptual abilities—traits that every business prizes.

Synchronize the Parts of the Brain

Your brain's complex system works best when all of its parts are synchronized in harmony. Imagine a championship basketball team that functions best when the five players on the court move in harmony. The center gathers the rebound, the forward takes it down the court, and the guard fires it through the hoop. When your brain's parts function in harmony, flashes of insight are embellished by quick memory recall of key details and then shaped by the neocortex (the analytical center of the brain), resulting in an innovative solution. Although scientists do not fully understand the way all the complex regions of our brains perform together to reach a creative insight, they do know that our sharpest perceptions occur when the various centers of our brain become synchronized. Heartfelt emotion helps harness all of the brain's centers in a way that allows us to solve problems with the utmost creativity.

The Institute of HeartMath, a research organization in Boulder Creek, California, has been exploring the connection between the heart and the brain for over 19 years. Their research studies have appeared in numerous peer-reviewed journals, such as the *American Journal of Cardiology, Stress Medicine, Preventive Cardiology,* and the *Journal of the American College of Cardiology.* Much of their research has been aimed at determining the heart's role in synchronizing the parts of the brain. Among other findings, they have discovered that the heart continuously connects with multiple centers of the brain via multiple routes: (1) electrically through two sets of nerve pathways; (2) electromagnetically by radiating a signal that reaches every cell in the brain; and (3) mechanically through pressure waves conducted along blood vessels. These pathways enable the heart to impose rhythmic patterns onto various areas of the brain. Sufficient rhythmic patterns get the parts of the brain in sync.

Think of your heart's rhythmic patterns as ocean waves. Just as the currents and winds and tides affect the height of the surf, so do our emotional states determine the pattern of the waves emitted by our hearts. Different emotions cause different patterns. For instance, anger and frustration cause an erratic and incoherent pattern. One second the sea looks calm; the next it rears up and crashes onto the shore. In contrast, sustained heartfelt emotions, such as boundless delight, unbridled appreciation, and tremendous gratitude, generate a smooth pattern with consistently high peaks and deep valleys, much like the big surf at Honolua Bay Beach.

Having extensively tested a broad range of people in all sorts of circumstances, HeartMath researchers have found that distinct heart patterns closely correlate with particular emotions. That makes it possible to use the heart's activity to measure a given emotional experience.

The high-peaks-and-deep-valleys pattern generated by heartfelt emotions send an effective synchronizing signal to the brain. Just like big waves in the ocean have a strong impact on moving a ship, the deeper wave pattern of heartfelt emotion has a profound influence on the brain. In fact, heartfelt emotion can facilitate a system-wide shift in brain functioning. Just like a basketball team that functions best when the players get "on the same wavelength," this global shift generates a state of mental optimal functioning as all of our cognitive and perceptual systems begin working in harmony.

HeartMath uses the term "coherence" to describe the state in which all of the centers of the brain develop a logical, orderly relationship. Coherence suggests a high degree of harmony and stability in mental and emotional processes. Heartfelt emotions such as deep appreciation, compassion, or love establish coherence. Our heart quite literally influences our mind.

When team members experience heartfelt emotion, their creative ability ratchets up a notch. That's why primal team leaders try to deepen team emotion. Suppose a team at Faraway University has set up a new system that allows the faculty to conduct classes for students at remote locations. The system displays these students on a large screen and allows them to communicate with their classmates as if they were sitting in the same room. What does the primal team leader do? She picks a few students in the remote location to show the team how dramatically the new system has enriched their lives. One student, a mother of three small children who has enrolled in an English-as-a-second-language class, tells the team that they have made it possible for her to gain valuable job skills while not leaving her kids with a babysitter. Her heartfelt gratitude delights the team and activates their heartfelt emotion. This helps the team achieve coherence, with waves of energy moving from their hearts to their heads. Of course, this creates a state of mind that will help them come up with their next big innovation.

Love, Coherence, and Creativity

Countless times I have seen coherence, sparked by heartfelt emotion, boost cognitive performance and prompt creative solutions to even the most perplexing business problems. I particularly recall watching a team working on an online auction site that needed a major software upgrade in order to make it more customer-friendly. But the team could not turn off the application while they worked to improve it because that would cost sales and irritate customers. Without going into the technical details, the team activated their heartfelt emotion and figured out an ingenious way to upgrade the system without turning it off. That sort of coherence enhances abstract thinking and broadens our scope of perception. In a state of coherence, new understandings and novel insights flash into our minds. We begin to see possibilities that previously eluded us. What once looked like a dead end suddenly appears to offer a promising path to success. It happens all the time, no matter how simple or complex the situation.

In this era of Big Data, where avalanches of information threaten to bury us alive, we need to find a way to cut through all the noise and find the clear signal necessary for us to do our work better. Coherence aids that quest. Not only does it enable us to recall information that we have committed to memory, it helps us mentally sift through large amounts of data to pinpoint the most relevant facts we need to make the best decisions. It works for individuals; it works for teams. In a team environment, coherence creates a condition in which every mind connects to a realm beyond the limits of each individual's capability. Insights arise that no one had previously glimpsed or imagined.

How often have you seen teams struggle with complex decisions? We often have to weigh complicated alternatives. Once again, coherence comes in handy because it increases intuitive clarity and the ability to discern reality. It clarifies the meaning of our flashes of insight. It helps us discern the real consequences of a decision or action and thus saves us a lot of time chasing wild geese or dealing with the unintended consequences of an unwise decision or action.

Suppose my team has to develop a highly intuitive interface for a smart phone application. When team members reach a state of coherence, their intuition, working memory, and analytical ability all work in harmony. Their minds stop jumping from one thought to another, their scattered thoughts coalesce, and their thinking and working grow more orderly and focused. Ideas for new features come immediately to mind, details of prototype feedback they had stored in their memory rise to the surface, and the accuracy of their predictions of the users' reactions to the interface increases. All parts of their minds and memories are working in harmony.

Work environments often create the high stress and troublesome interpersonal problems that undermine a team's sense of confidence. Here again, coherence saves the day because it enhances a team's sense of well-being. One particularly enlightening HeartMath study involved the Information Technology Services Division of a state agency, which was implementing a major technology upgrade that required employees to learn new skills. Not only did the new platform challenge the employees' sense of mastery and security, but changes in leadership also added uncertainty regarding the organization's direction and future. All of this made most employees angry, resentful, and anxious.

Wisely, the leaders of the organization hired trainers to teach breathing techniques that helped employees instantly transform emotional negativity into a state of coherence. The techniques specifically aided employees in accessing their innate self-confidence by removing the layers of stressful negativity. When the employees learned how to reach a state where they felt collected and capable, they gained and maintained more confidence, even in the midst of a stressful environment. They now felt as though they could handle whatever challenges came their way. Confidence makes people feel hardy and resilient. When the going gets tough, the coherent team perseveres past every obstacle. When change comes along, the team adapts swiftly and effectively. Using the right techniques, team leaders can help their people adapt to major change and get their work done without a major hitch.

In contrast to coherence, negative emotions such as fear, anger, worry, and anxiety can severely limit learning, memory, cognition, and problem solving. Negative emotion leads to poorly thought-out or shortsighted decisions, difficulty finding the right words and remembering key facts, slowed reaction speeds, and a paralysis caused by events that overwhelm us. We find ourselves in a state of confusion that scientists call cortical inhibition. People and organizations in this state can't compete effectively. Such inhibition stems not only from outbursts of anger or extreme anxiety but also from all the little daily hurts and worries about the future that a team experiences.[6]

DAMPENING THE ENERGY

When I first began leading large teams, I believed that making them happy would make them successful. I spent a lot of time listening to what people wanted and giving them what they said would make them happy: a casual dress code, a strong voice in decision making, a telecommuting option, and flexible work hours, to mention a few. But all that effort ended up with my getting bitten on the hand.

My intense focus on making everybody happy created an environment where people spent way too much time thinking about what they wanted and then complaining when they didn't get it. It all came to a head one day during a heated discussion about whether managers or their reports should make certain decisions. Some employees argued that team members who actually did the work should make most of the decisions. Others insisted that a top-down approach would speed up decision making and avoid a lot of time-wasting discussion among team members. We could see no easy solution to this problem and ended up with a compromise, which meant that nobody was really happy with the solution. The teams felt frustrated, the energy of the group faded, and the creative juices dried up.

Then one day Derek, an extremely vocal systems analyst, said, "I am so unhappy with the way decisions get made around here." His words turned on a lightbulb in my head. Of course! No approach would make everyone happy because different people want different things.

Explode the Myth of the Happy Workplace

A March 2013 *Harvard Business Review* blog contended that when organizations create happy workplaces, productivity improves.[7] Who can argue with that? People in good moods solve problems more creatively. But you can't make an entire organization happy any more than you can fit everyone into the same size sneaker. If you try to do that, you will end up with an inbox full of complaints from people who hate black shoes and suffer from sore feet. The factors that lead to happiness come in a broad range of styles and sizes.

According to Jaak Panksepp, an American psychologist and neuroscientist who has conducted extensive research on emotional systems, unique conditioning triggers each person's happiness. In other words, your personal experiences shape the high-level cognitive emotion we call happiness. Such cognitions occur within higher neocortical brain regions that receive all the unique input you experience during your life. What tickles me may nauseate you, and vice versa. I like snakes because my brother kept a pet python in his room; you hate snakes because a diamondback rattler bit your mother on a golf course. Monica wants the boss to make all the decisions; Derek wants to make all the decisions himself. This applies to every aspect of the work environment.

I now know that leaders should not try to achieve happiness in a whole team or organization. Rather, they should concentrate on simply optimizing the more primal emotions we all share, such as playfulness and the desire for new experiences. These emotions arise from the lower regions of our brain (e.g., the thalamus and hypothalamus) and get passed along naturally. They exist regardless of our unique experiences.[8]

I'm not knocking happiness. I've seen it pervade a whole team. When it does, you get amazing results. However, striving to make everyone happy will end up making *you* unhappy. Happiness may mean different things to different people, but optimal heartfelt emotions don't.

Conventional Practices

On the plus side, the concept of happy workplaces acknowledges that optimal emotions can help people get good results. Most organizations have the cause-effect loop backward. They work hard trying to achieve success so that they'll feel good, without realizing that feeling good must come first in order to achieve success.

Two other management best practices also respect emotion as a precursor for success: emotional intelligence (EI) and employee engagement. A whole industry has sprung up around EI, which, among other things, recognizes that people in positive moods do a better job. Engagement, which revolves around the notion that success hinges on getting people thoroughly involved in making the organization a success, also stresses the importance of strong positive feelings and attitudes. Although you can use both of these practices to help shape positive employee emotions, you should recognize their limitations.

A December 2001 *Harvard Business Review* article titled "Primal Leadership," written by emotional intelligence guru Daniel Goleman, proposes that an effective leader must maintain a consistently optimistic, high-energy mood. Employees' moods depend heavily on the leader's emotional state. You'll find a lot of useful techniques for modeling the right behavior in all of Goleman's books.[9] So what's the downside? If Laura plays the "happy clown" to Fernando, jolly and affable on the outside but sad and coldhearted on the inside, she merely *displays* rather than *feels* the positive emotion. Fernando can sense the mismatch. Worse, Laura can suffer from the effects of emotional dissonance, a state in which her emotional display differs markedly from what she really feels. Maintaining the façade can take a huge emotional toll on Laura, resulting eventually in burnout or emotional numbness.[10]

In the case of employee engagement, the leader strives to motivate employees to invest more discretionary effort in their work by instilling in them a strong desire to help the organization. However, leaders too often attempt to shape employees' emotional desires by giving them *logical* reasons to want the organization to succeed. They paint a picture of how employees' jobs fit into the organization's overall strategy, they articulate why the company has a bright future, and they offer logical reasons why everyone gets paid exactly what they deserve. Those leaders who practice the lead-by-logic approach mistakenly believe that reason drives emotion. In fact, as we will see throughout this book, you can more effectively create the state of mind you desire by working directly with emotion.

Let the Good Feelings Roll

The idea of creating happy workplaces, mastering emotional intelligence, and forging engagement acknowledges the power of emotion in business and the need to optimize it. But the notion of inviting emotions into the workplace repulses many leaders because they find emotions so messy, sticky, gooey, and frustrating. Such leaders would rather ignore than nurture their people's primal natures.

Unfortunately, the very way businesspeople think tends to diminish the positive emotion in workplaces. When something happens at work that evokes happiness or joy, we often downplay those feelings. When we attract a major new client, we say, "Our advertising department really does a good job." When we set a new sales record, we say, "Our Widget simply outperforms the competition." Psychologists use the term "ordination" to refer to this tendency to make exceptional events seem ordinary. Instead of just letting ourselves feel personally delighted over our role in wooing a new client or selling a million Widgets, we use cool logic to explain the event and diminish our reaction to it. Logic trumps delight.

A predictable and explainable event elicits a less intense emotional reaction than a novel and unpredictable one. Because ordinary events command less intense feelings than extraordinary ones, we do not remember them as vividly. Straight-and-narrow businesspeople prefer the predictable and explainable because predictability breeds consistency, but if you emphasize consistency, you rob events of their intense emotional power. They become less dramatic, and thus less memorable, and consequently less influential on the team's emotions.

The inclination to ordinize events comes so naturally to us that we seldom give it a second thought.[11] Primal leaders understand this human tendency and look for opportunities to encourage a team to revel in the joy of accomplishment.

When your team does something wonderful:

- **Rejoice.** Stay emotional rather than minimizing the event with logical explanations. *"Wow! We hit the one million mark! Amazing!"*

- **Celebrate.** Commemorate the event. *"This marks a milestone not just for our team and company, but for the whole industry. Lunch at Joe's Grill on me!"*

- **Exclaim.** Show your emotion, telling people how it makes you feel. *"I can't tell you how happy this makes me. I feel like the day we brought my newborn daughter home from the hospital."*

GOING TO THE SOURCE

Tyler, a team leader at Saelco Industries, trudges into the office, worrying about his job. His boss, Liz, has asked him to stop by and chat about his team's weakening performance and deteriorating morale. Although Tyler works hard on his leadership skills and his team likes him a lot, he can't control a lot of what's happening at Saelco.

Upper management keeps changing technologies, priorities, and staffing levels, all of which undermine his team's sense of mastery and security. To make matters worse, a constant merry-go-round at Saelco's top executive level keeps adding uncertainty about the organization's direction and future. All of this keeps Tyler's team feeling resentful and anxious and underperforming.

Liz opens her meeting with Tyler by insisting he make a compelling business case for all the changes. "Look," she says, "the company's moving in the right direction. I'm counting on you to *sell* it to your people and get them back on track." After the meeting, Tyler tries every persuasion technique he knows, but nothing works.

Then one day Tyler comes across an article in a trade journal that explores the topic of primal emotions in the workplace. He realizes that fear and negative emotion have consumed his team and that no amount of cold hard logic will ever conquer those feelings. He makes it a point to learn a couple of emotional self-management techniques that will help his team shift into an optimal emotional state.

Each day for a week, Tyler convenes a 15-minute team meeting in which he guides the group through a three-step exercise designed to shift their emotions to an optimal state:

1. **Stop.** Invite everyone to erase thoughts from their minds. As Tolstoy famously observed, if you tell someone *not* to think about a polar bear, they can't get polar bears out of their heads. Tyler says he likes to picture a perfect tomato in his mind's eye. Concentrating on that round, red, juicy object pushes other thoughts out of his head.

2. **Breathe.** Ask them to focus on the area around their heart and to imagine breathing into their heart for about 10 to 15 seconds. Tyler closes his eyes and demonstrates how to do this: in ... one-two-three, out ... one-two-three.

3. **Activate.** Urge them to conjure up a positive feeling, not just picturing it in their mind, but *feeling* it with their entire body. Tyler explains how a genuine heartfelt emotion feels, and he tells them how he felt when he and his wife brought their newborn daughter home from the hospital.

After a few weeks of setting aside time to elicit heartfelt emotions, Tyler sees a visible change in his people. They smile more often, laugh a lot, and obviously enjoy each other's company much more than they did a few weeks earlier. Liz also notices a new vitality in Tyler's team. Everyone seems freshly energized, exuding much more confidence and enthusiasm. Best of all, they're coming up with solutions rather than dwelling on problems. Liz takes Tyler aside one morning and says, "I don't know how you did it, Ty, but you've turned your gang around." He just smiles. He realizes he can't always convince his team that they should understand and like what's happening in the company, and he certainly can't guarantee a fabulous future. But he can help them feel good about themselves and their teammates and prepare themselves for whatever comes their way.

Make Emotional Shifting a Daily Habit

Over those few weeks, Tyler taught his team how to self-manage their emotions by instructing them to use the Three-Step Emotion Shifter technique regularly, making it a habit to relax for a moment, to think-breathe-visualize. However, he went beyond the conventional practice that centers on the head when he went straight to the heart. By involving his team's hearts, he could more surely move them into a state of coherence where optimal emotions could help them get better results.

Coherence and a state of optimal emotion, Tyler knows, do not fall on people like rain; people must make their own rain. Anyone can learn how to spot problematic negative emotions that suppress peak performance and replace them with positive ones that promote success. This works no matter what's happening within the team and its environment.

Tyler wanted the team to go beyond *recalling* a past heartfelt emotion like carrying your baby daughter into your house and to feel a genuine heartfelt emotion here and now. He emphasized the somatic, or body-based, sensations involved.

As his people make emotional shifting a daily habit, they facilitate a repatterning of their brains and nervous systems and become increasingly familiar with how it feels to work in a more constant state of coherence. Optimal emotions become more firmly established in their neural architecture. Good feelings and coherence become the new normal.

Record Biofeedback in a Coherence Journal

Some of the people on your team may find it hard to grasp the rather abstract and elusive concept of coherence. For them, you can make it more tangible and real with the use of biofeedback devices that can measure a person's state of coherence in real time. You can obtain these relatively inexpensive little machines from many sources, but I can personally vouch for a product called an emWave offered by HeartMath LLC. While your team practices shifting his or her emotions, each team member can attach a clip to an earlobe or place his or her thumb on a sensor. They then receive signals that reflect their level of coherence. A green light indicates a state of coherence, and a red one reveals a flatter or more negative emotional state. In addition, a lively bell tells them they've reached a state of coherence, and a dull buzz means they have not gotten there yet. Once the team members see the green lights and hear the jingling bells a few times, they can recognize whether they're reaching it or not in subsequent sessions.

Your team can even record their coherence levels over time by attaching the biofeedback devices to their computers. That way, they can see a graphic, real-time display of their coherence level, which they can log into a personal Coherence Journal. Over time, this diary of responses to daily working situations can tell them a lot about when and how they reached a desired state of coherence. Before long, they'll find it much easier to reach and maintain that state while tackling a major issue.

HeartMath researchers have tested similar techniques in many business and government organizations, from information technology teams in state agencies, to health care providers in for-profit hospitals, to church pastors. Some of the organizations were suffering through stressful changes at the time, and others were simply experiencing the day-to-day emotional ups and downs of the typical workplace.

The results show that people can and do learn to self-manage their emotions in stressful situations, quickly transforming their emotional states to a more positive place and evoking a coherent state at will. Amazingly, they do it without disrupting their work activities.[12]

Tyler's group quickly learned how to shape their emotions. However, most other teams, steeped in the tradition of downplaying emotions in the workplace, will find it much harder to do. In the next chapter, we will learn even more about shifting emotions at the source.

USING AN EMOTIONAL SAVVY GAUGE TO MEASURE YOUR TEAM'S EMOTIONAL PROFICIENCY

Before you move on to Chapter 2, try using this exercise to gauge your team's skill at dealing with emotions. You can apply it to individual team members as well as to the team as a whole. Think about the six ways individuals or the group at large tends to cope with emotions. Which approach best describes their typical stance? Each approach springs from a basic assumption or belief. The way team members talk about an issue provides a clue to that underlying belief.

You can roughly rank your team's emotional know-how on a scale of 1 to 6 (1 meaning you need to make some serious improvements to the way your team handles emotion and 6 meaning you can feel pretty good about your team's emotional proficiency).

1   2   3   4   5   6

1. **Evading Emotions.** Belief: The business will run best without any messy emotions; all conversation should stick to cold hard facts. *"I don't care if the team is feeling anxious and stressed. They just need to meet the schedule and come in under budget."*

2. **Confusing Causality.** Belief: Only success can make people feel good; success does not depend on feeling good. *"If we deliver the project on time and on budget, that will make everyone happy."*

3. **Controlling Behavior.** Belief: You should manipulate your emotions to keep them positive all the time. *"Yeah, the project is three months past due and 50 percent over budget, but I'm optimistic that it's all going to turn out well in the end."*

4. **Applying Reason.** Belief: Logic trumps emotion. *"Employees should recognize that no matter how stressed they feel, this is still a great place to work because we have a solid compensation package and a compelling strategy."*

5. **Shaping Feelings.** Belief: You can reduce negative or stressful emotions. *"Now that we've put that intense shareholder's meeting behind us, let's take a few deep breaths to calm down. We can get back to a happy place."*

6. **Vitalizing Hearts.** Belief: We work best when we activate heartfelt emotions every day. *"We finally delivered the project on time and on budget because we paused every day to shift our emotions to an optimal state."*

CHAPTER 2

Primal Emotion

Shifting Emotions at the Source

When smart phone maker WidgeComm recruited Laura Turner to streamline the company's supply chain, she tackled the assignment with boundless enthusiasm and energy. She could not have asked for a more skilled team of technicians than the one WidgeComm had assigned to the project. But it didn't take long for her to realize that her team did not share her enthusiasm. She felt her optimism swirl down the drain the day Nick, her most senior analyst, frowned and said, "This is just one more in an endless line of projects. I'm sick and tired of the long days and tight deadlines."

Despite the ambitious goals set for the team, Laura noticed that everyone dashed out the door at five o'clock sharp. After a few sleepless nights, Laura decided she'd do something about her team's lack of enthusiasm. She thought back to her management training. What would management guru Peter Drucker counsel her to do? "He'd tell me that I need to find out what makes each person tick and put some carrots on the end of the stick to lure them." However, Laura knew she lacked both the time and the budget to do that. What would emotional intelligence expert Daniel Goleman advise? "He'd say I need to get the team engaged in jointly crafting an inspiring mission statement." Laura could just imagine Nick and his colleagues smirking and rolling their eyes if she suggested *that*.

Then she got a bright idea. Why not loosen people up with a more playful office environment? With nothing to lose, she turned the team break room into a playground, with her son's old Xbox Playstation, a foosball table that she found in WidgeComm's storage room, and several Native American drums. Hoping this new space would ignite positive emotions and high-energy play, she urged the team to take frequent breaks in what Nick jokingly called The Fun House. Sure enough, within a week, the fun spilled over into the workroom. Finally, people were beginning to display a new sense of eagerness and optimism. Even Nick often kept working long after Laura had left the building at six o'clock.

Why did playing games boost the team's enthusiasm for their work? Because Laura's team had been suffering from an *emotional,* not a work, issue. Burnout had battered their energy and arousal levels. When a team's energy hits rock bottom, you can only cure the ailment by striking at its source.

Our emotions spring from the primal parts of our brain. Basic and instinctive, they date back to the time when Mother Nature hardwired them into the base of our brain as we learned what worked and didn't work in our ancient environment.

When neuroscientist Jaak Panksepp, whom we met in Chapter 1, led a team that surgically removed the higher, analytical portions of the brains from various experimental animals at birth, they discovered that those animals grew up to lead emotionally normal lives. This phenomenon also occurs in young humans born without the higher regions of their brain. It implies that we can work more directly with emotional feelings through basic body dynamics and instinctual tendencies, rather than with analytical logic.[1] When Laura engaged her team in play, the physical activities positively affected their emotions and reduced feelings of burnout.

One primal emotional system plays a key role in one of the most crucial aspects of human behavior in business: motivation. In this chapter, we'll look at some techniques that will help you build optimal emotions in your team and pep up their drive.

USING NOVELTY TO REIGNITE DRIVE

Driving home from my soccer practice one evening, I listened to a radio interview with a member of the mime troupe, the Blue Man Group. He told the interviewer that during his first year with the group, he could not believe his good fortune. He had landed the best job in the world. It wasn't work at all but a deeply gratifying way to apply his artistic and creative talents and have a ton of fun at the same time. However, although entertaining huge crowds tremendously energized him, after performing several hundred performances, he found his mind wandering on stage. He'd catch himself contemplating dinner or shopping for groceries. Why in the world would a fellow with the best job in the world eventually grow bored with it? Even if I love my job, I wondered, will I too eventually find it less than fulfilling?

It turns out that even the most creative people lose some of their energy once they've made their great discovery or built the next-generation product. Obviously, it poses a serious problem in business when a group that possesses boundless energy at the beginning of a project loses a lot of its momentum before they have accomplished their objective. Fortunately, there are ways to counteract boredom and burnout and reignite a team's energy and enthusiasm.

Motivate at the Deeper Level

Whether you want to inspire your team to come up with the most creative design for a supply chain or you have to pump up the troupe to wow an audience, you need to provide ongoing motivation. Yet motivation, like love and truth and beauty, remains elusive. We can't define it precisely, but we know it when we see it. Why does Chou work happily at his desk long after midnight, while Nick seldom puts in more than his minimal 40 hours a week? The reason is not always easy to explain. You can't make emotions completely concrete and tangible. So when we talk about motivation, we must approach it not as a logical problem but as an emotional issue.

Traditional team leaders try to motivate their people by presenting the cold, hard *facts* with statements like, "You should care about and invest high energy in this work for this reason." However, no two people work for exactly the same reason. Take Laura's team, for example. Chou, who grew up with three competitive brothers, wants to outdo his siblings by moving up the corporate ladder and making lots of money. Burton grew up with an absentee workaholic father and will do everything he can to avoid working late and losing valuable time with his kids. Wendy fell victim to downsizing at two previous employers and worries about polishing her resume for her next job. Laura has three unique individuals with three vastly different motivations on her hands. Figuring out what makes them all tick takes a lot of time and skill because most people cannot clearly articulate what motivates them the most. *Why* does Chou work so hard? *Why* does Nick slack off so much? Why do *any* of these teammates do what they do?

Even if Laura takes the time to fathom what makes each team member's motivational clock tick, she must still wrestle with a tight budget (no big raise for Chou), a demanding schedule (more overtime for Burton), and inflexible roles (fewer new skills for Wendy). But even if she could magically give all her people what they really want, she must deal with an even more fundamental problem.

Many employees simply lack the additional energy you want them to put into their work. Bestow all those raises, protect your people's home lives, give them a chance to acquire exciting new skills, and you still end up with people suffering from burnout or boredom who just can't handle one more straw on the camel's back.

That's when a smart leader applies emotional solutions. Such solutions do not require more resources. They just depend on one fact unearthed by Jaak Panksepp's team of neuroscientists: at their basic emotional level, Chou and Burton and Wendy share a lot in common. Dr. Panksepp's research supports the fact that our fundamental emotions arise from the ancient lower regions of our brain, which are instinctual. That region does not differ much from individual to individual. Therefore, leaders can much more effectively shape emotions directly at this lower region than they can at the higher-brain logic level.[2] You need to reenergize Nick and Chou and Burton and Wendy. Don't appeal to their intellects. Get them involved in a rousing foosball tournament, lead them in a drumming circle, or give them a good laugh when you get booed off the stage playing Guitar Hero. I've seen this approach almost instantly boost the energy and creative ability of a team. It happens around the foosball table, on the field during the softball game at the annual company picnic, and in the break-room-turned-game-room. Vigorous play and joyous laughter can quickly revitalize energy and create more vigor for work in the whole team. Rather than waiting until a team reaches burnout to pep them back up, primal leaders incorporate play and laughter into their daily leadership practices.

Seek Before You Find

Jaak Panksepp's research indicates that we get a bigger thrill from the chase than from the capture. The very act of chasing, seeking, or pursuing the wild boar motivates us much more powerfully than cooking and eating it. Chou may think that a bag of money makes him work hard, but deep down it's the pursuit of success that really turns him on. Note the subtle distinction here. Yes, the money provides an attractive lure, but swimming toward the lure sparks Chou's energy. The Blue Man finds himself drawn to entertaining an audience, but once he has delighted them time and time again, the act loses some of its charm. Once we attain a goal, win a prize, give a customer the experience of a lifetime, or bring a new Gizmo to market, we find it less interesting and want to move on to the next shiny lure. We all share a "seeking" emotional system, which arouses our emotions and governs our motivation. The new shiny lure ignites it. Stephen Crane's poem "A Man Saw a Ball of Gold in the Sky" captures this idea perfectly:

> *A man saw a ball of gold in the sky;*
> *He climbed for it,*
> *And eventually he achieved it—*
> *It was clay.*
>
> *Now this is the strange part:*
> *When the man went to the earth*
> *And looked again,*
> *Lo, there was the ball of gold.*
> *Now this is the strange part:*
> *It was a ball of gold.*
> *Aye, by the heavens, it was a ball of gold.*

You get a thrill out of pursuing or seeking a goal, but once you achieve it, it doesn't seem so attractive.

What does this mean for the team leader? First, you should bear in mind the extreme pleasure people derive from activating their seeking emotional system. In laboratory tests, animals will make self-stimulating their seeking emotional system an overriding priority. Jaak Panksepp and other researchers working with him have set up experiments where laboratory animals with electrodes implanted in their brains can self-stimulate their seeking emotional system by pressing a button that applies electric jolts to the brain region responsible for this emotion. When the animals can choose between stimulating their seeking emotional system or eating to stay alive, they will choose the former. Although we humans may not starve ourselves for the thrill of the chase, the chase still figures prominently in our behavior. Just think about the thrill you got when you did something amazing for the first time, such as driving into Yellowstone Park or getting off the subway in Manhattan to catch your first glimpse of the Empire State Building. Your heart rose as you felt a strong sense of wonder and joy. The same happens to teams. Achieving this optimal emotional state powerfully motivates people. But after initially seeing Old Faithful erupt or the sun glinting off the skyscraper's spire, subsequent viewings lose some of their luster. If the experiences become a daily routine, they eventually become as routine and boring as doing the same job day after day after day.

Knowing this will happen, Laura takes care to create frequent novelty for her team. If she can keep stimulating her people's seeking emotional systems, she can keep them motivated to excel at their work. Nick and Chou and Burton and Wendy may remain convinced that certain specific rewards spur them to do a great job, while they actually get their greatest inspiration from a hot new project that will afford a lot of fresh, exciting experiences.

Now this is the cool part: When a stimulus arouses our seeking system, it activates our frontal neocortex, prompting us to work out innovative strategies and solutions. Logic doesn't make us do that; emotions do. The brain's neocortex, the source of our human analytical intellect, serves our emotions, not vice versa. A team that embarks on an exciting new journey not only feels strongly motivated to succeed but also works smarter.

When our seeking system comes to the party, we feel as though we can accomplish anything. Negativity evaporates; fear takes a vacation. We feel confident we can conquer the world.[3]

Use Novelty to Invigorate

The opportunity to pursue or experience something new jazzes people. Think about it. How did you feel the first day you strolled into the office and began your new job? Did you feel on top of the world? What about a few months or years later? Did you feel as though you were going through the motions, putting another square peg into another square hole? I bet you did, unless, of course, you regularly encountered novel experiences (star-shaped holes, round holes, dazzling new colors) that kept your enthusiasm running at a high level. Primal team leaders know how to do that.

If you happen to work in a high-tech company, you may encounter novelty every day. In this age of disruptive technological innovation, today's whiz-bang gizmo becomes tomorrow's obsolete gadget. Keeping up with or racing ahead of the curve automatically boosts a team's energy. Other industries should be so lucky. Take a warehouse job, for instance. Imagine how long it would take for you to get bored stiff driving a forklift around all day. How do you inject novelty and freshness into a team engaged in work that changes at the speed of a glacier?

If I took charge of a team working at a warehouse, I'd try to keep people feeling fresh by periodically shifting their responsibilities. I'd transfer Don from driving a forklift to running the shipping/receiving desk and move shipment expediter Tom into that slot. The change of scenery and routine will spark a little more energy. Yes, each must learn a new role, but learning itself fulfills the appetite for seeking novelty, and the extra enthusiasm sparked by doing something new should more than make up for any loss of productivity caused by traveling the learning curve and getting up to speed in a new job.

I might also engage my people in process improvement initiatives, which provide great opportunities for them to get involved in new and different work. During the slow periods during his workweek, Don can spend a few hours designing a more effective system for handling special requests. The chance to do something new and interesting that will streamline a cumbersome process can get his creative juices flowing. He's happier. The warehouse workers are happier. Customers are happier. I'm happier.

Organize Work in Creative Cycles

Other primal team leaders have learned to maintain a high level of enthusiasm by organizing the work in creative cycles. The movie industry provides a great example. Within the span of a year or so, people join together to envision and plan the next blockbuster, create it in a relatively short period of time—say a year—and then disband with feelings of satisfaction over completing the project. The next project soon gets them back on the enthusiasm track. No one suffers from tedium and boredom because the work occurs in patterns that keep it fresh. One month you're planning the sets and selecting the actors and designing costumes; the next month you're filming scenes, and the next you're editing the footage. Phase 1 gives way to phase 2, and phase 3 follows on the heels of phase 2. Then the next project refreshes the pattern. The clear beginnings and endings provide the excitement of starting something new and the fulfillment of completing the work.

Any work involves certain patterns. A leader can use this fact to keep team energy running at a high level. For instance, when Laura's team develops the new supply chain software, they progress through certain creative phases not unlike making a movie. The team envisions the application they need to create, they assign team roles, they write the code, they test the result, and then they install it. Whatever your business, you can break the work into similar creative phases.

Let's say you run the Information Technology Group at WidgeComm. Team A supports the current systems to keep them running smoothly. Every day they monitor and make small adjustments to the applications. That work can get pretty dull. Team B builds and implements brand-new systems. That team almost certainly feels more engaged than Team A. Perhaps you could rotate people in and out of the two teams. A Team B player will initially find Team A work interesting, whereas a Team A player will feel excited over doing something new with Team B. You might also move some Team A work to Team B, incorporating some of the patches into the creative cycles of the projects. That way, more people get the thrill of working in patterns that boost the feeling of freshness and novelty. Team A wins. Team B wins. The department wins. And the team leader wins. The leader made it all possible by looking at the work in terms of phases and cycles and adding variation to the equation.

What happens if, despite all your efforts to introduce novelty by managing phases and cycles, boredom creeps into the team? The body, not the brain, can best answer that question.

PLAYING FOR THE FUN OF IT

The team of four Apple engineers who developed the first Mac computer in 1979 knew how to play. They worked in a space filled with enough toys to make it look like a geeky child's playground: remote-controlled vehicles, balls in all shapes and sizes, and hanging nets. All in good fun, someone would bean a teammate with a Nerfball, prompting a lively game of tag. To defend against attack, everyone surrounded their work area with cardboard blockades to protect them from flying objects. Soon they had turned the area into a makeshift maze.[4]

If you had asked that early Mac team about their workspace, they would probably have told you they just wanted to relieve stress with a little harmless fun, but they had unknowingly engaged in one of the best activities to boost their creativity. Yes, the play did reduce their stress, and, as scientists have learned, playing even strengthens areas of the team's brains that previous stress may have damaged. However, it did a lot more than that. It optimized their emotions by making them feel positive and aroused. It also fueled their seeking system, ensuring keen motivation and emotional resilience. If you love your new iMac or Airbook or iPad, chalk it up in part to Nerfball tag. A silly game enabled the team to handle the emotional ups and downs of their mercurial boss Steve Jobs and build a machine that turned Apple into the most highly valued corporation on the planet.

Play in the Optimal Way

Like all those balls in the Mac team's workspace, play comes in a lot of different forms. Some forms of play, such as training for a marathon, feel like work. Other forms, such as a rousing game of tag or a game of Marco Polo in the swimming pool, feel totally fun and pleasurable. The latter kind can best ensure a team's optimal emotional state.

The most effective type of play involves physical repetitive actions with certain variations, such as throwing or batting, that challenge us enough to attract and hold our interest but that do not overly tax our minds and bodies, as training for a marathon does. Ideal play should enhance rather than sap our energy. Contrary to the old cliché, winning is *not* everything. The mere act of playing the game for the sheer fun of it, without excessive pressure to win, *is* everything. That's why a game of Nerfball tag worked so well.

A word of caution: Some team leaders try to turn the work itself into play. "I'll give a day off to the programmer who finds the most bugs in the software this week." That doesn't work because that sort of game involves significant consequences for the winners and losers. It can do the opposite of rejuvenating a team's emotions.

Perhaps you have tried some of the recently popular gamification techniques, such as awarding points or badges to people who solve a customer's issue or come up with a great idea. Gamification techniques seldom qualify as optimal play, although they may offer other benefits (like making the work more interesting and motivating people to achieve the rewards).

Even though optimal play does involve multiple players, it should not prompt competition for rewards, achievement, or status. For optimal play to work its magic, the strongest players should willingly handicap themselves to make sure everyone can enjoy playing on a level field. When the strongest players don't exhibit this kind of reciprocity, the fun drains out of the game for the other players. Muscle-bound Nick may excel at softball, but if he plays hard only to win, petite Laura and uncoordinated Wendy will wander off to find a more enjoyable activity. But if Nick will only bunt the ball when he comes up to bat and walk rather than run the bases, he will level the playing field and make everyone laugh.

Play becomes most beneficial when every participant's motivation and emotional arousal run high. The game must invite everyone to perform well. Even with his handicaps, Nick will try hard to help his team score runs. Laura will rise to the occasion with a fervent effort at first base, and Wendy will do her best to stop a ball that reaches her in the deep outfield.

Another word of caution: There's a big difference between the sort of optimal play we're discussing and overly structured activities. Optimal play erupts spontaneously. Laura knows that the predictable and highly structured softball game the company plays at noon sharp at every annual picnic always makes Wendy's heart sink. Rather, Laura just asks Nick to bring a ball and bat to the park, then during a lull in other activities, she asks whether anyone wants to play a three-inning game. If the group does not respond enthusiastically, she might suggest games everyone remembers from childhood. "Anybody up for a game of Kick-the-Can?" With my own teams, I have found ping-pong quite effective. In any event, I like to set aside a few hours every quarter to do something fun, perhaps a scooter race or pumpkin carving contest, but I also encourage spontaneous outbreaks of ping-pong or other forms of fun and frolic. My people know I love to do that—within reason, of course.

Release the Inner Child

Adults who dismiss playfulness as a childish trait miss out on the great benefits it can deliver, especially in business environments where managers and leaders want people to take their work seriously. Even if you feel uncomfortable with childish games and would never consider playing Kick-the-Can, you can still invite play into the workplace.

As we humans mature, we tend to replace playful physical engagements with verbal jousting. Wendy pokes a little good-natured fun at Nick's bulging biceps, and he retorts that he's glad he doesn't trip over his own shadow the way she did trying to catch that fly ball to deep right field. Friendly teasing and verbal jousting can create the same effect as physical play, but you need to know where to draw the line. Teasing can easily descend into bullying, and an overly sharp verbal dart can pierce the target's heart. When verbal play crosses the line, it can do the same damage as unfettered I-win/you-lose competition, which brings us to a third and crucial caution: Treat teasing and verbal banter like a bottle of nitroglycerine. Handled gingerly, it can stir up a team's positive emotions, but dropped on the floor, it can blow up the whole department.[5]

Verbal banter works best when the people involved know each other well. Laura knows from her hiring interview with Wendy that she pokes fun at herself over her clumsiness, but if you make a joke about her skinniness, she will blush and nurse the wound for days. Nick needs to know that before he teases her that a little gust of wind would blow her back to Kansas. On the other hand, he quite enjoys it when Wendy teases him about his physique, in which he takes great pride.

SOUNDING OFF

Scottish regiments of the British army have traditionally marched into war to the sound of bagpipes. Although many people may shrink at the wail of the bagpipes, Scottish soldiers hear it as a rousing call to arms. The most celebrated bagpiper of World War II, Bill Millin of 1 Special Service Brigade, piped his unit onto the Normandy beaches on D-Day. As Millin waded onto Sword Beach, playing "Road to the Isles," he kept piping despite all the cacophony of bursting shells and whistling bullets. He kept it up as his unit triumphantly fought their way to their objective, Pegasus Bridge. When his unit reached their objective, Millin piped the troops across the bridge under the withering fire of German snipers.[6]

Music can inspire accomplishment when fear or burnout threatens performance, but it can also "soothe the savage breast" during times of great stress. According to Dr. Michelle Lefevre, Senior Lecturer in Social Work and Care at the University of Sussex, the pitch, tempo, and melodic pattern of music influence the listener's mood and physical processes. High pitch, accelerated rhythm, and ascending melodic passages generally increase emotional arousal and tension. That's why Millin's bagpipes inspired his unit to accomplish its mission. On the other hand, music with low pitch, slow tempos, and descending melodies usually decrease the listener's level of arousal. Laura keeps a compact music system in the workroom. When she senses fear or burnout creeping into the team, she cues up the classic rock playlist with a lot of danceable tunes; when she sees stress causing a bit of frantic behavior, she switches to Beethoven and Brahms. "You should have been a DJ, Boss!" jokes the usually dour Chou.[7]

Bring Out the Musician in Everyone

Listening to music affects a team's emotions, but making music stimulates them even more. In a study led by Barry Bittman, and reported in *Alternative Therapies in Health Medicine*, researchers found that when people *participate* in a group drumming exercise, their bodies show significant signs of improved health. Merely listening to the drumbeats does not affect them as much.[8]

If you and your people can engage in a game of Nerfball or Kick-the-Can, you can surely learn to bang a drum or play a kazoo. We're not talking about opening at Carnegie Hall. We just want to inject a little percussion or tooting into the workplace. Few people can master the viola or bassoon, but almost anyone can get into group drumming activities. Tapping on bongo drums and rattling tambourines bring people together physically, emotionally, and mentally. It takes no advanced training, involves inexpensive instruments, and transcends cultural, age, and ethnic backgrounds. Start with a simple tune that might create the desired effect, perhaps "Row, Row, Row Your Boat" to boost everyone's spirits or "Amazing Grace" to tone them down.

Of course, the folks who shy away from childish play may initially resist participating, but it never takes long for even the most hardboiled curmudgeon to join in the fun. When Laura suggests a ten-minute drum fest, Burton rolls his eyes and asks her to excuse him because he needs to finish a report. Three minutes into the session, he picks up a snare drum and starts beating it in tune with the others.

Forget about everyone playing in pure harmony, however. You're aiming at fun, not a Gold Record. When less than well-coordinated Wendy goes offbeat with her drum, Nick does the same. The ensuing cacophony makes everyone laugh out loud. Whatever instruments or tunes you choose, emphasize camaraderie, group acceptance, light-hearted participation, and nonjudgmental performance.

Researchers have confirmed that group drumming can alleviate burnout in a work environment. An article published in *Advances in Mind-Body Medicine* describes a study led by Barry Bittman that tested the effect of music on the moods of 125 long-term care workers at Wesbury United Methodist Retirement Community in Meadville, Pennsylvania, many of whom who were experiencing burnout.

Subjects met with a trained facilitator for an hour a week for six weeks. During the sessions, the facilitators asked the participants to perform simple drumming exercises that reflected their emotions. At the end of six weeks, the researchers found that the subjects had achieved a significant reduction in emotional exhaustion, anxiety, and fatigue, as well as a measurable increase in vigor and personal accomplishment.[9]

If you think drumming in the office sounds nutty, think again. Employees at government, health care, and community organizations and several big companies, including Toyota, Unilever, Raytheon, and Oracle, regularly participate in drumming activities at work. Toyota has gone so far as to install dedicated "drum rooms" at the company's California locations.[10]

Let Music Stimulate Self-Expression

When people uniquely express themselves, instead of just following the leader, a musical activity becomes even more consuming and powerful. Blazing your own trail always excites you more than tagging along behind someone else.

Unique expression can begin with instrument selection. For the drumming circle, Laura's team chooses instruments that match their personalities: Burton picks up an Indian clay pot, Chou a Native American drum, Wendy a triangle, and Nick a big bass drum (of course).

Once your team has mastered basic drumming, progress to something a bit more complicated, such as a call-and-response exercise. This allows for further self-expression. First the group establishes a basic foundation rhythm. Then each person in turn adds a new simple rhythm, which the rest of the team repeats.

Depending on your team's musical talent and training, you can add more instruments and create more elaborate music. I will never forget how Jim, a fairly skillful guitarist on a large applications development team, would coordinate a team concert once a year. He sweet-talked even the most tone-deaf teammate to play along. One such fellow, Jay, recited the words in King Tut style, imitating the classic Steve Martin skit from the late seventies. Other musically challenged people, like me, danced or shook the tambourine.

Music rejuvenates our basic emotional system, reinvigorates our urge to play, and inspires our natural inclination to seek.

LAUGHING OUT LOUD

Laughter is not only the best medicine, it's the best measure of fun in the workplace. Some people react to a good joke with a belly laugh; others chuckle under their breath. Still others force their laughter, even if they don't find the joke funny. When it comes to authentic laughter, you know it when you hear it.

Laugh Yourself Healthy

According to the Mayo Clinic, when you laugh, it doesn't just lighten your mental load; it induces measurable physical changes in your body.

You breathe in more oxygen-rich air, your heart beats a little faster, your muscles tingle, and mood-enhancing chemicals called endorphins flood your brain. An authentic laugh fires up and then cools down your stress response while increasing your heart rate and blood pressure, and you enter the emotional target zone of positive feelings and moderate arousal.[11]

According to an October 2011 article by Carolyn Butler in the *Washington Post*, the benefits of laughter are more prevalent when people vocalize their laughter and the muscles all over their body contract.[12] While Nick's body-quaking hearty laugh works wonders, Wendy's gentle chuckle that makes her raise her shoulders and clap her hands also moves her toward the desired state.

If your team includes a natural-born jester, congratulations. But there's no law against you and your teammates developing a stronger sense of humor by listening to comic performers and scouring the Internet for good jokes appropriate to various occasions. Laura used this one before a team meeting: "How many programmers does it take to screw in a lightbulb? ... None. That's a hardware problem."

Know What's Funny

Laughter, like playfulness itself, instinctively arises from the lower regions of our brain.[13] That argues for keeping humor simple and basic, like Laura's joke. Remember, you're appealing to emotions, not intellect. For this reason, funny faces and quirky exclamations often elicit the most boisterous laughter. When Burton from Georgia wants to make the team laugh, he starts talking in his most exaggerated Southern drawl. That cracks everybody up.

Not everything cracks everyone up, however. A long, involved shaggy dog story may require listeners to engage their higher-level analytical minds, which vary from person to person, depending on individual conditioning. Wendy was bitten by a dog as a child, and Burton is bitter about never having a dog, so they don't find a story like that funny.

Also keep in mind that an audience generally reacts more favorably to self-directed humor than to jokes at someone else's expense. The team always laughs when Nick jokes about his physique, but not so much when he pokes fun at 300-pound Burton's weight.

If you just can't learn to tell a joke, don't despair. Dancing and other types of bodily activities can create optimal emotions just as effectively as a good belly laugh.

LETTING YOUR FACE DO THE TALKING

Back in the 1990s, Paul Ekman, an emeritus professor of psychology at the University of California at San Francisco and a world authority on facial expressions, studied human facial expressions in an attempt to learn whether you could read people's emotions merely by looking at their faces. Not surprisingly, the Federal Bureau of Investigation, the Central Intelligence Agency, and many state and local police forces drew on Dr. Ekman's research to help them detect subtle emotional cues on the faces of potential assassins, terrorists, and suspicious visa applicants. One day, Ekman and a colleague were exploring the expression of anger and distress when they realized that after making angry faces all day, they felt terrible. Just frowning, it turns out, can make you sad, not just vice versa. The researchers' angry faces created significant changes in their autonomic nervous systems and generated real feelings of anger and distress in their hearts. Heartbeats went up and hands grew warm, even though the researchers were just doing a normal day's work.

They then experimented with other subjects, telling one group to remember and relive stressful experiences, while asking another group to assume a series of specific facial expressions they did not know reflected angry feelings. Both groups exhibited the same physiological symptoms.[14]

Ekman's discoveries highlight the fact that you can shift your emotions and those of your teammates with amazingly simple techniques.

Smile and Be Happy

It really works. But it takes more than an upward curl of the lips to raise your spirits. To generate the physiology of true happiness, you must also move the muscles around your eyes. It turns out that anyone can turn on feelings of anger or disgust just by making a face that telegraphs those emotions, but no more than one in ten people can fake a smile that looks genuine. Unless you feel truly amused, excited, grateful, relieved, or just plain happy, you probably can't pull your cheeks up and your eyebrows down to form a smile that looks genuine because that involves certain *involuntary* muscles.[15]

When I needed some professional PR photos last year, I worked with a photographer who taught me how to look genuinely bright and cheerful. Rather than telling me to say "Cheese!" before she snapped a shot, she asked me at the beginning of the session to name a couple of people who always made me feel great. I named my husband, Jim, and my good friend, Gretchen. Then when she wanted to capture my expression, she told me to say, "Hi, Jim" or "Hi, Gretchen" and imagine that person actually walking into the room. This simple act gave me a jolt of true happiness, which brought forth a genuine smile. I both looked and felt happy. Try this trick yourself. It can help you shift emotions in the wink of an eye.

How many different kinds of smiles can you make? In addition to the genuine happy variety, Paul Ekman counted 17 types of smiles, which he described in his 1985 book, *Telling Lies*. Most of them express negative emotions, such as fear, horror, or embarrassment.[16] We've all seen that nervous smile when someone does or says something regrettable. It takes practice to call up the happy smile, especially when you're feeling quite the opposite.

A June 25, 2012 *Psychology Today* blog by Sarah Stevenson discussed how flashing a genuine smile physically influences your brain. Smiling activates the release of neuropeptides, tiny molecules that allow neurons to communicate and work together in an effort to ward off stress. These molecules tell the whole body that we feel happy. Your body releases the feel-good neurotransmitters dopamine, endorphins, and serotonin when a smile flashes across your face as well. This not only relaxes you physically, but it can lower your heart rate and blood pressure. A smile-induced serotonin release brought on by your smile serves as an antide-pressant and mood lifter.[17]

Smiles shift emotions at the primal level. The world may keep falling down all around you, but a real smile will make you feel better about it. Laura's team has fallen hopelessly behind schedule on the big project, the computer network has crashed, Burton has brought a nasty flu bug into the office, but they can still slap on a happy face if even for a moment and feel better about their work. The positive effect will persist long enough to get the team back on track.

Grin and Bear It

What other methods can Laura and her team use to generate the smile effect? An article by Robert Kraut in a 1979 issue of the *Journal of Personality and Social Psychology* sheds some light on why people smile. When Kraut studied the conditions under which people smiled while bowling, he found that people readily smiled when shouting, jumping, and gesturing after bowling a spare or a strike but smiled much less when they bowled a high score with no one present or had not yet turned to face their team. Smiling, it seemed, depended on social contact, looking at or talking with their teammates. In that context, bowlers would even laugh and joke with the team if they threw a gutter ball.

Why does social contact promote smiling? Perhaps participation in a group makes people happy. Or maybe we just like to display our good feelings in the presence of others. Either way, this research provides strong evidence that social involvement significantly increases the frequency of smiling. You may smile in response to a hilarious joke, but you will smile more broadly if you hear it in a group setting.[18] Laura had heard Nick's joke about programmers changing a lightbulb before, but at the pizza parlor after the softball game, she laughed so hard she practically fell off her stool.

Encouraging a lot of face-to-face contact among your team can have a beneficial effect, even if you can only do it on a Skype conference. Burton and Chou convene a weekly conference call with their primary software vendor, but instead of doing it on a shared phone line, they meet in the conference room where they can look one another in the eye while chatting with the vendor. When Chou shares a joke only a software designer would get, they all enjoy a hearty laugh. The optimal emotions they experience carry over into their work later in the day.

The shortest way to a lover's heart may be through the stomach, but it's also the quickest route to a smiley face. When Burton walks through the team room carrying a box of Krispy Kreme doughnuts or a barrel of Kentucky Fried Chicken, the whole team breaks out in smiles and jumps up to follow him into the break room, even skinny Wendy, who normally eats like a goldfinch.

And don't get me started about cute kittens and puppies. Why do you see so many pictures of them on the Internet? Almost no one can resist smiling at a bundle of puppies wrestling in the clover. I remember the time when our team lined the office walls with photos of their beloved pets. Everyone smiled when they saw Steve's fabulous photo of his cat sitting on a fence, rubbing noses with a llama. Imagine our reaction if he ever brought the charming critter to work. Some companies allow that on a regular basis.

And flattery will not only get you everywhere, it will elicit a great big smile on the recipient's face. Everyone gets a kick out of hearing praise for a new hairstyle or an exceptionally bright idea. Avoid false flattery, however, because people can easily detect faked admiration. During a recent consulting engagement, I watched a video a client named Eric had created to teach nontechnical employees how to use a new software tool. The video wouldn't win any Academy Awards, but Eric appeared totally genuine on screen. When I complimented him on his screen presence, he smiled as if I had just given him a new BMW for his birthday. A heartfelt thank-you makes the same magic. Everybody appreciates appreciation and will usually acknowledge it with broad smile.

USING THE EMOTION SHAPE SHIFTER TO MODIFY EMOTIONS AT THEIR SOURCE

You can consult the summary of the techniques described in this chapter in The Emotion Shape Shifter in order to select ones that might get the best results for your team. They fall into three distinct categories: (1) embellishing the teams' office environment, (2) enhancing the team's communication style, and (3) enriching work practices and processes.

The Emotion Shape Shifter

Office Environment	Communication Style	Work Practices and Processes
Use toys and games to create an inviting place to play.	Inject humor into conversations and meetings.	Organize work in creative cycles.
Provide a variety of percussion instruments.	Laugh at yourself.	Use process improvement to counter boredom.
Install a music player and select a wide range of tunes, from somber to ecstatic.	Engage in verbal jousting.	Shift responsibilities periodically.
Offer tasty treats from time to time.	Encourage compliments and appreciation.	Encourage breaks to play or make music.
Line the walls with lovely, stimulating, or amusing photos.		Bring the team together face to face.

CHAPTER 3

The Scary Stuff
Processing Fear and Negativity

Early in my career I was working in a new management position at a company we'll call Acceleric, a large logistics company in the Pacific Northwest. Still quite young and inexperienced, I found myself struggling to maintain my composure with my brightest employee, Roger, who had tendered his resignation after accepting a plum job with Expedite, one of Acceleric's archrivals. "You *can't* resign," I pleaded. "You're running our largest projects." Roger lifted his eyes from the floor, shrugged, and said, with noticeable excitement in his voice, "They're giving me a huge salary increase and a nice signing bonus. Plus, I get to use the new design tools from Oracle!"

I felt crushed. I took it personally. What had I done to drive him into the arms of a competitor? Though headquartered in Los Angeles, Expedite had set up its technology center across town from our offices in Seattle. Obviously, they had made that move in order to raid Acceleric of our best and brightest people.

Fearing that this setback could destroy everything I had worked so hard to build, I went into an emotional tailspin. I had handpicked my technologists, courted them to join Acceleric, and invested heavily in their development. If they left, I'd find it extremely difficult to replace them. What had happened to the strong relationships that I had worked so hard to build? Was I fooling myself? Was I just an incompetent boss?

I began losing sleep over this crisis and found it harder and harder to concentrate at work. People in our office began to quarrel over insignificant issues, leaving the office early, and avoiding eye contact with me. My performance and the performance of my team suffered to the point where I began to worry about losing my job. Instead of motivating me to work smarter and harder, fear had paralyzed me to the point where I could see only doom on the horizon.

Business environments swarm with fear. When everyone competes for limited resources, both with other companies and with the person sitting in the next cubicle, every project turns into a win-lose contest. Just consider the language we use in these situations: "competitive threat," "defensive maneuver," and "risk management." When a key teammate departs and our best-laid plans fall apart, fear burrows even deeper into our hearts. No wonder I couldn't sleep at night.

Our emotional system reacts to perceived threats to our survival by producing responses that maximize our chances to survive the threat. Negative emotion tends to dominate these responses. You are swimming 20 yards from the shore when you see a big fin pop out of the water between you and the beach. Your mind is flooded with images of severed limbs and blood in the water. You may try to flee or fight the shark, or you may just freeze. This occurs just as surely when you think you see a threat to your business or career. You might choose to run away or battle the threat, or you might just freeze, as I did when Roger quit.

In Chapter 1, we explored how anger, worry, and anxiety severely limit cognition and creativity. We also examined techniques for shifting such emotions from negative to positive, but can or should we always do that? Sometimes negative emotion can be used to our advantage.

Knowing how to process fear and negativity can turn a potentially damaging problem into an opportunity for positive team development.

Fear can strike a team for any number of reasons (an impossible deadline, the sudden departure of a teammate, a hostile takeover of the company, or any dramatic change in upper management), but you can always take steps to prevent fear and negativity from impeding peak performance. In this chapter, we'll explore ways you can release a team from the claws of fear and stimulate higher performance.

ACCOMMODATING NEGATIVITY

Outspoken and aggressive, David Weiss, a web developer at General Engines, has always voiced strong opinions about the look and feel of the company's website. When his manager, Nancy Colletto, informs his team that she cannot approve their urgently needed budget request, David loses his cool. Turning red in the face, he shouts, "This company doesn't give a damn about the customers who visit our website. They'll take one look at our old stodgy design and go looking for a smarter supplier." His teammates just squirm uncomfortably in their chairs.

David's outburst ignites Nancy's own anger. She had pushed so hard for the increase that her own boss told her to back off and go back to her people with the business case for a flat budget. She feels like someone has put her head in a vise. Taking a deep breath, however, she smiles and calmly says, "I understand your frustration, David. I feel exactly the same way. Look, we're in this together. Why don't we show them we can pull a rabbit out of the hat?" She goes on to explain why the company can't afford to invest more in web development at the moment. Eventually David grins and holds up both hands. "Hey, I just can't stand it when competitors beat us to the punch with smart new web features. But I've got a couple of ideas that won't cost another dime." Freshly energized, the team begins to brainstorm how they can get the most out of their current funding.

In most business environments, David's teammates would not have tolerated his outburst. His uncontrolled display of anger would have earned him a reputation as a bad team player and could have done irreparable damage to his career. Yet no one on a team should expect people to control their emotions 100 percent of the time. Trying to do that can cause its own set of problems.

Stop Fostering Detachment

When that shark fin surfaces a few feet from you, you cannot stop fear from jangling your brain. Input from our emotional systems affects our cognitive systems much more swiftly than vice versa. Strong emotions quickly override our logical thinking and prevent our rational minds from ordering our fear, anger, or anxiety to go away. Emotional responses occur instantly, before our cognition can possibly intervene. Not even David's keen intelligence could stop him from instinctively lashing out when he felt threatened by insufficient resources.

Such involuntary responses to a threat began forming long before humans emerged from their caves. David responded the same way his ancient ancestors would have reacted to a saber tooth tiger popping out of the woods.[1] But in his case, a natural response to a perceived threat could have posed grave danger to his career. Lucky for him, Nancy knew how to deal with such emotional displays and turn them into a positive force.

Most employees don't risk such emotional outbursts. Instead, they tamp down their emotions by reducing their emotional attachment to their work. Highly engaged employees form deep emotional attachments to their work. They feel deeply passionate about doing a great job and getting excellent results. When danger strikes, they naturally experience equally strong negative emotions. By disengaging, they reduce the chance that their emotions will cause problems when something scary happens. It's a lose-lose proposition. The employee loses the spark that leads to stellar performance; the employer loses the great results, innovations, and creative solutions it needs to succeed in a tough competitive environment.

Wisely, Nancy kept David engaged by allowing his outburst, then skillfully shifting his focus from the negative to the positive. She used his strong engagement to help solve the problem that set him off in the first place.

Start Capturing the Benefits of Negativity

We can take another important lesson from the way Nancy handled David's negative emotions. While the team surely felt discomfort over David's eruption, the incident did bring certain benefits to the situation. Despite the intensity of his outburst, he expressed some valid concerns. His rage rang a loud warning bell that the team should address a real and immediate problem: creating a fabulous website with limited resources. An unemotional, dispassionate response could have easily gone unheard. When the threat appeared and the alarm sounded, the team tackled the threat with gusto.

The expression of negative emotions can spark a team from lifelessness to alertness. Optimal mental functioning depends on emotional arousal because emotions contribute greatly to attention, perception, memory, and problem solving. Without emotional arousal, we can fail both to notice important danger signals and to muster enthusiasm to address the threat.[2]

Make Room for Negativity

Teams cannot capture the benefits of negative emotions unless they feel they can safely express them without getting criticized or punished. A leader must deliberately create this safe space because most people assume that expressing strong negative emotions in the workplace will get them in trouble. A safe haven should include specific rules that draw a line between acceptable and unacceptable behavior.

It usually takes some time for a team to grow comfortable with this approach. The team leader must invite people to share their emotions and explain why doing so will help the team improve performance. Just as no question is a stupid question, no emotion is a bad emotion. Some people will find expressing themselves without fear of consequences easy to do; others will take some convincing. Make sure you allow for individual differences. While outspoken David may get it right off the bat, it may take a lot of encouragement for reticent Eve, a coworker, to get on board. You can also model the acceptable expression of negative emotion by regularly and openly sharing your own feelings.

NANCY: Forgive me while I bang my head against the wall over this setback.

[Nervous laughter breaks out around the table.]

DAVID: Yeah, it really pisses me off, too.

EVE: I lost sleep over it last night.

NANCY: Okay, let's let it all out and then put our heads together to figure out how we can wow customers with the new website.

What if Eve bursts into tears during the discussion? Early in my career, I would cringe whenever a woman (or occasionally a man) would cry at work. I considered it taboo, something that a businessperson absolutely never does, no matter what. But over the years, as I studied the role of emotions in the workplace, I came to accept a broader range of emotional displays. David yells his head off. Okay, that's just David being David. Eve sobs into her hands? That's Eve for you. The trick is not letting either display hijack a meeting or drive the team toward a bad decision, just to make David stop shouting or Eve stop bawling.

Despite the proven benefits of negative emotion at work, we've all seen them metastasize and create emotionally toxic work environments. How can we make sure that such poison does not spread throughout the team?

SHINING A LIGHT ON FEAR

As a leader of technology teams, I've seen a lot of fear in the eyes of employees. Every day, companies outsource entire departments overseas;

every minute, hard-earned technology skills become obsolete; and every second, senior leadership cancels a major project and disperses a team. I recall an especially memorable team meeting when fear stalked the room. A critical project had fallen badly behind schedule, and I needed everyone's full attention. When I showed up a few minutes early, I noticed some team members sitting slumped in their chairs at the other end of the table. Unobserved, I heard one of them mutter, "They're a bunch of blithering idiots." Another offered a high five and said, "Yeah, how can they be so stupid," while a third snarled and said, "I've got a gerbil with more brains." When they saw me, they smiled sheepishly. "What's going on, guys?" I asked. One of them smirked. "Another data center in town is being outsourced. If this trend keeps up, we're going to be standing in the unemployment line."

Fear of losing their jobs had infected and demoralized the team. No wonder they'd fallen so far behind schedule. I knew our company wasn't planning to outsource our data center, but I couldn't promise it would never happen. So I met the fear head-on. When the rest of the team showed up, I said, "Okay, people. The threat of outsourcing is real, so take it seriously. But it's not going to happen tomorrow." I did not add that we stood a better chance of losing our jobs if we didn't get this project back on track. Did substantiating their fear create more worry? No. Why didn't I just say, "Forget about it and concentrate on this project"? Because I knew that acknowledging a potential threat brings it into everyone's consciousness and makes it far less distracting.

Make Threats Conscious

Our emotional system, the region of the brain called the amygdala in particular, continuously scans our surroundings for potential threats and then warns our conscious mind when it detects one. It's part of our survival instinct. We're always subconsciously looking for clues that signal danger. Someone around us may casually say "outsourcing," and our amygdala sends a warning that puts our body on red alert. "Danger! Danger! You will lose your job!" If our conscious mind ignores or denies the clamor, our emotional system keeps sounding the alarm. This keeps our amygdala so active that we can scarcely concentrate on anything else.

Not only does the amygdala warn us of possible danger, it also heavily influences our thinking. If we detect a looming threat, our amygdala fires up, keeping us highly aroused until we determine the true nature of the threat. It can shift our entire brain into withdrawal mode, where we can think of nothing else. This can cause us to look at the world through a distorted lens that interprets every ambiguous event as a possible danger. We hear about another company outsourcing jobs and jump to the conclusion that the same thing is going to happen to us.

Acknowledging a threat surfaces it into our conscious mind where we can process it, which is why I used this Acknowledge the Threat technique with my team. Once I confirmed everyone's suspicion that bad news could arrive at any time, their conscious minds agreed they could do nothing about that threat but that they could do something about the work at hand. If our conscious mind acknowledges the threat and either takes precautionary action or decides to let it slide, our amygdala can take a break and stop sounding the alarm.[3] When the team sees the situation through a clearer lens, they can get back to work.

If I had tried to squelch the conversation and refocus the team on the troubled project, I would have done nothing to reduce their fear. They would have bottled it up inside, where it would only keep festering. Those internal warning bells would keep clanging. Work would grind to a halt. We'd end up with pink slips in our shaking hands.

Although acknowledging a threat does not make it go away, it does allow room for a conscious intention to stop worrying about it now and resolve it later. It tells our emotional system to chill out. If necessary, we'll get hot about it later.

Talk About the Pain

Now let's look at a situation where an individual's personal experience makes it hard to concentrate on the immediate work, even after consciously acknowledging the threat. Imagine a talented new recruit I'll call Padmasee. I hired her after she had been laid off by her previous employer during a radical downsizing initiative. The same thing had happened to her more than once in her career. It took her a year to connect with me, and by that time she felt completely shell-shocked. The mere inkling that she might lose this job scared her to death. What do you do when acknowledging a threat does not calm someone's amygdala? You talk about it.

Just talking about feelings disrupts the effect of the amygdala. However, when you encourage others to articulate their feelings, you want to steer the conversation away from what is prompting the fear. Instead, you get someone like Padmasee talking about how it feels to worry about losing a job. The very act of describing how we feel activates another part of our brain, which disrupts and dampens the amygdala's influence. I call this the Tell Me Where It Hurts technique. It might go like this:

MANAGER: When you worry about losing your job, where do you feel it in your body?

PADMASEE: I feel like I can't breathe, and my stomach burns. Plus, I feel such a heavy weight that I can barely move my feet.

MANAGER: What goes through your head when you worry?

PADMASEE: I keep wondering if it's something I've done. Maybe it's my fault somehow, but I can't think of how. But mostly I just feel sad and deflated.

MANAGER: I was laid off my job once, and I felt defeated and helpless.

PADMASEE: Yeah, I'm feeling pretty down and discouraged.

MANAGER: Please come and talk to me anytime you're feeling down. We could make it part of our morning routine. Really, there is a light at the end of the tunnel, and it's not a train coming to smash you flat.

PADMASEE: Ha-ha! That's the first time I've smiled all week.

Encourage others to go into specific detail about their feelings, beyond such generic descriptions as "bad" or "good." Persuade them to expand their emotional vocabulary by providing some examples of vivid descriptors: "frightened," "depressed," "desolate," "empty," "panicky," "petrified," and "disgraced," to name a few. Ask them about the physical effects of their emotions. Does their pulse race? Have they lost their appetite? Do they toss and turn at night? Do they feel a burning sensation in their stomach? Thinking about their physical responses to situations helps them find the words to describe their emotions.

When getting others to talk about their feelings, don't try to regulate or modify their emotions. Encourage them to talk openly without suggesting that they may be overreacting or that they really shouldn't fret. Remember that you want people to grapple directly with their emotions without judgment or the interference of their cognitive processes.[4] Let logic take a vacation while raw emotions bubble to the surface.

At the beginning of a meeting in which you want to surface emotions, ask for an emotional check-in. Go around the room and encourage each person to share his or her true feelings. Not only does this help alleviate the effect of any disruptive negative emotions, it gets the team accustomed to expressing emotion. Of course, you also want to invite people to open up emotionally whenever you sense fear, anger, worry, or plain old grumpiness. In any case, delay discussion of substantive work issues until all participants have vented their feelings.

CREATING A DIVERSION FROM NEGATIVE THOUGHTS

The employee portal on Merck's intranet abounds with stories about the pharmaceutical giant's efforts to create a healthier planet. One video stars Michele Baldwin, a cancer patient Merck sponsored to paddle the

Ganges River in order to promote the importance of screening for cervical cancer. Another posting highlights Merck's pledge to donate Mectizan, a medicine that halts the debilitating symptoms of river blindness, to those who need it in South America and Africa.[5] This content doesn't just motivate Merck's employees; it also helps them deal with fear.

What makes Merck employees fearful? During the past few years, some of the company's most lucrative patents have expired, and new patents have not yet offset those losses. As a result, the company has cut thousands of jobs.[6] The positive visuals of the good Merck does in the world helps employees shift into peak performance. When team members recognize a threat like possible layoffs, they naturally experience negative emotions that threaten their productivity. Emotionally uplifting stories and visuals help people replace their negative thoughts and emotions with the more positive ones they need to perform well at their jobs.

Understand Working Memory

Although scientists lack a full picture of how human consciousness works, they do agree on a few basic principles. Our cognitive and emotional systems constantly process a vast array of stimuli, yet most of that processing occurs below our conscious awareness. Our brains can hold only one *conscious* thought at a time. That thought arises when the system responsible for conscious awareness becomes privy to an activity occurring at the unconscious level. Cognitive scientists often call that one conscious thought our *working memory*.

The conscious mind will award priority to an emotional stimulus. While your mind unconsciously processes all stimuli, it grabs emotional stimuli, especially negative ones, faster than others, and it brings them into your conscious awareness. When we see the shark circling our little raft, our minds snap to attention as the defense networks of the amygdala flood our working memory with information about the threat.

Once our conscious mind latches onto a negative or fearful thought, it can exclude everything else. We spot the shark in the water and immediately forget about tomorrow's client meeting and next week's deadline for a big deliverable. Working memory focuses on the shark as it tries to figure out what to do about the threat. Our cognitive deduction and decision-making processes, controlled by working memory, become tightly focused on the fearful situation. Employees who start thinking about a real or imagined round of layoffs worry a lot more about losing their jobs than about doing them well.

Both the mundane stuff of everyday life at work (addressing a minor customer complaint, for example) and the really intense high-voltage worries that strike from time to time (anxieties about job security) can seize control of our conscious minds, but the intense ones easily bump the mundane ones aside. We leave the customer hanging while we fret about our future, or, more commonly, we put a half-hearted effort into satisfying the customer because we can't let go of our fear of losing our job. Again, it's a lose-lose situation. The company loses a customer, and we may lose our job due to lackluster performance.

Enliven the Positive

We naturally find it hard to replace a negative thought with a positive one because we're predisposed to latch onto the negative. It boils down to our hardwiring. Our brains will naturally respond more rapidly and powerfully to the scary stuff than to the happy stuff.

Because nonemotional events, even positive ones, do not easily push aside strong emotional ones, you can't expect your team to hold more positive thoughts in their consciousness if you do not build an *emotionally* positive work environment.[7] In the case of Merck employees, the powerfully strong positive reminders that the company does so much good in the world helps them more easily shift their conscious focus away from possible layoffs. The positive images and stories, with their accompanying strong positive emotions, embed themselves in working memory. Team leaders who wish to create positive emotions with the power to boot out the negative will find this Accentuate the Positive technique quite useful.

Arouse Positivity

Most of us know what makes teams fearful, but what arouses positive emotions? It's telling that the research on our fear emotional system is prolific, yet there's very little research on how our positive emotional systems work. Once again, we are obsessed with the negative. So in answering the question of what evokes positive emotions, we have to rely largely on intuition and deductive reasoning.

Rocks and other inanimate objects, even gold coins and dollar bills, evoke less powerful emotions in us than interactions with other people. Strategic plans and revenue charts, no matter how compelling or upward-trending, can never fire up our emotions as much as a story about how our team efforts improve our lives and the lives of others. Objects are cold and hard and lifeless; people's lives are messy and sticky and compelling.

A team's work can touch lives positively through the content they provide, such as Merck's medicine, or they can do it through the context of their work, such as using sustainable products that preserve a fragile planet. Either way, the more vividly you can describe the positive impact of your work on peoples' lives, the more you will populate your teammates' working memory with positive thoughts. Identify the most compelling way in which your team makes lives better, and define it in a way that elicits strong positive emotion.

All successful businesses and their teams provide valuable content to their customers. Not every team pursues an unusually noble and life-saving purpose like Merck's, yet every team leader in every business can define a purpose that will evoke positive emotion. We'll learn how to do that in Chapter 6.

Some teams may find it easier to feel more positive about the way they operate than about the service or product they provide. I once worked with a team who wrote software for analyzing the profitability of nuclear power plants. Although many of us felt a bit leery about the content we were providing, we enjoyed a great team culture that honored each person's input and unique abilities. The context of how our team operated provided a compelling way to keep our thoughts positive.

Keep It Visible

Once you've defined the best way to create positive emotions in the team, use symbols to keep it visible in their minds. Make the symbols vivid and tangible, so that people can picture them in their mind's eye. Merck uses storytelling to depict the value of the company's product. Our software team decorated the walls with pictures of ourselves and our families to remind us why we work so hard to get results.

In her book *The New Corporate Facts of Life*, management consultant Diana Rivenburgh describes visiting a Novo Nordisk plant in Clayton, North Carolina. Most of us know Novo Nordisk as a company that makes drugs for people suffering from diabetes. As Diana strolled down a long hallway connecting two buildings, she marveled at a wall painted the same vivid blue color as the pharmaceutical company's logo. Named "The Blue Mile," the wall displays large photographs captioned by the stories of diabetics and hemophiliacs whose lives have been made healthier and happier through the use of the company's products. The company leader accompanying Diana proudly pointed out that these photos depict family members of Novo Nordisk employees. The wall aligns the people at Novo Nordisk with a higher purpose that fills their minds with strongly positive thoughts and emotions.[8]

Keep refreshing the symbols. Over time, team members grow bored with the same old symbols and no longer notice them. When Novo Nordisk revitalizes its symbols, people keep dropping by to read new stories. My software team also hung new eye-catching pictures of our families to keep our dedication fresh in everyone's mind.

Divert the Cognitive Brain

Cognitively challenging tasks can also divert the brain from negativity. Get the team to develop a solution to a puzzling problem or to perform any activity that requires deep mental engagement and concentration. Quite often, teams must accomplish daunting tasks that everyone would rather keep avoiding. With what I call the Occupy the Brain technique, you can distract a team from negativity while they perform daunting tasks. For instance, I have assigned tasks like these to divert a team from negative thoughts:

✓ Develop improvements to the team's most complex process.

✓ Figure out how to solve a difficult customer request.

✓ Determine the best way to measure the team's performance.

✓ Complete an ROI assessment for purchasing a new tool set.

Although this technique helps shift the team's focus away from negativity while they concentrate on the task, be aware that it will not provide long-lasting benefits because once they complete the task, those emotions will resurface. Plus, the bad feelings can seep back into their brains as the task wears on. You'll have to use some of the other techniques to get sustained relief from negativity.

DESENSITIZING YOUR TEAM TO FEAR

Francois Baker, a computer analyst at lighting manufacturer Bright-World, flinches as the system alert flashes on her computer screen. Almost simultaneously, she hears the moans of her teammates in the surrounding cubicles. The planning system has crashed, and her team will get all the blame. She quickly checks the system statistics, praying that they'll reveal something she can easily fix. But no such luck. None of the team has ever seen this problem, and their initial triage doesn't give them a single clue about the cause of the disaster.

The planning system outage begins wreaking such havoc with operations at BrightWorld's 300 manufacturing locations around the globe that the team cannot read all the angry emails cramming their inboxes. The phone rings constantly. Francois has never heard such loud swearing. Everyone on the team feels shell-shocked. They sit at their desks like zombies, unable to think the problem through.

Knowing she must do something to get everyone back to work on the problem, Francois herds the team into the hallway between their cubicles and says, "Let's feel the weight of our situation. All of our locations are down and everybody in the field hates us." Her teammate, Mark, adds, "We're losing credibility by the minute." The team visibly writhes with pain as they let themselves feel the full brunt of their emotions—all the shame, embarrassment, guilt, and an overwhelming sense of abject failure. Still, Francois makes sure they do not exaggerate the problem. When Mark moans, "We may never work again," the others tell him that's just not true. After a few minutes of emotional venting, Francois says, "Now let's all take a few deep breaths and recall how we all felt when we solved that outage a few months ago. Do you remember the relief and satisfaction? Let your body feel it. Now let's go back and fix this one." It works. Within five minutes, the whole group has returned to their computers, their fingers flying over their keyboards. A half hour later, Mark shouts, "Yay! I found the bug!"

Reprogram the Fear

Francois used what I call the Desensitize to Fear technique to help her team transcend fear. This technique includes a tried-and-true four-step Fear Prescription:

1. Face the full extent of the fear.

2. Avoid exaggeration or catastrophizing.

3. Conjure up the somatic effects (i.e., the way it makes the body feel).

4. Shift to the positive.

Fear and anxiety, especially in a business environment, arise because we believe that a threat will cause pain and suffering. Francois's team members link the system outage to feelings of shame or guilt or loss.

This association keeps their fear and anxiety levels so high they can't fully concentrate on their work.

In such a case, the manager prescribes an anesthetic that will desensitize the team to the fear. This technique works much like the extinction method psychotherapists use to help people overcome a debilitating fear.[9] If the mere sight of a snake crossing the road causes you to break out in a cold sweat and swerve your car off the road into the sagebrush, you might put a ceramic model of a coiled rattler on the floor beside your big flat screen television set. You'll see it while watching television every night, and before long you'll no longer associate the mere presence of a snake with pain and suffering. Voila! You have faced the fear and tamed it.

You can apply this prescription to the workplace. Of course, fear in the business world comes in more complex packages than a simple fear of snakes. In our work lives, we fear the pain caused by complex negative emotions such as shame, guilt, or embarrassment. We can also fear the pain of loss, be it the loss of status, financial security, pride, power, or anything else we highly value. We fear these emotions because we don't believe we can handle the pain they cause. However, when we face these fears head-on, letting ourselves feel the full brunt of the emotions they ignite, we realize that we really can handle the pain. That knowledge robs the emotions of their power to scare and immobilize us.

Francois sets up a situation in which her team can fully feel the negative emotions caused by the system outage, accepting them without diminishing them in any way. Before long, they realize that what they've feared the most won't destroy them, and thus they reduce the threat's ability to scare them to death.

Before you apply this prescription to your team, try it out on yourself. Pick your worst nightmare, perhaps going bankrupt and losing everything, not just financially but emotionally (loss of self-worth and self-confidence coupled with feelings of shame, regret, despair, etc.). Now, don't script a story about how you got so deeply in debt or how you can work your way out of it because that would keep the problem in your cognitive mind. You want to stay in contact with the unconscious level from which your emotions arise. Just *feel* it. Feel it some more. Keep feeling it. Those intense emotions should slowly dissipate.

Don't think of fear as your worst enemy. Don't fight it tooth and nail. Put your arm around its shoulder, take it for a walk in the park, and make it your friend. If the members of Francois's team had run away from their fear and never met it head-on, they would not have been able to buckle down and smoke out the bug that had threatened their careers.

Apply a Dose of Logic

I often recommend what I refer to as the Get Real technique when fear runs rampant in a team. To this point, our discussion has concentrated so much on processing fear directly at the emotional level that you may wonder about applying our rational minds to easing its effects. Although we may logically fear certain dangers in business, we often exaggerate the threats. Have you ever overgeneralized a bad event, turning one problem into a pattern of failure, completely ignoring any positives that may come from dealing with it? During the system outage, Mark said, "We may never work again!"—clearly an overreaction to the situation. When his team pointed that out, he changed the way he felt about the problem.

A team leader should keep a sharp eye out for exaggerations and outlandish consequences voiced by team members. Challenge their unwarranted fears, put them in perspective, and lessen their negativity with a dose of logic. Change their fear of catastrophe, change their feelings of despair: "No, that's not a rattlesnake; it's a harmless garden snake. It eats pests. Here, pet its back. It's not slimy, it's soft and pliant. It's not your enemy, it's your friend."

Strengthen Resilience

Although business environments swarm with events that may easily evoke fear and anxiety, we can build up our resilience to them. Don't wait for an emergency to build resilience. Begin building it in your team from the get-go. Then, when emergencies do present themselves, as they always do in today's rough-and-tumble business world, your team will keep its wits about them and apply their full cognitive and creative abilities to solving the problem.

Without resilience, teams not only react more fearfully to negative events; they actually experience fear of a wider variety of them. Frequent arousal conditions our emotional systems. If we experience a lot of fear, our fear emotional system grows more sensitive to a lot of events that would not have previously caused such a reaction.[10] Whenever a team lives in an almost perpetual state of fear, it will quite likely experience fear even when something rather innocuous happens. A field manager sends an email to Francois asking whether the system will keep working tomorrow, and she perceives it as a criticism and feels extremely anxious about it.

When we experience a lot of negative feelings, our brains signal our adrenal glands to pump more cortisol into our system. Excessive amounts of cortisol linger in the bloodstream for hours, maintaining our feelings of anxiety. We become jumpy, thin-skinned, and easily upset. We perceive more threats in our environment, and we react more strongly to them.[11] In contrast, when we experience a lot of positive feeling, our bodies produce more of the hormone DHEA, which gives us a natural sense of well-being, hardiness, and resilience.[12]

You want to get your team to inhabit a positive mental world where negative events do not make them fearful. What I call the Bounce Back technique accomplishes both. To use this technique, Francois leads a ten-minute exercise at every other team meeting. It goes something like this:

FRANÇOIS: What are your biggest fears about our work?

MARK: I'm afraid we're going to fail, disappointing all our stakeholders.

FRANÇOIS: Which emotions would that bring up for you?

MARK: The embarrassment of being incompetent.

KAREN: Also the shame and guilt of letting people down.

FRANCOIS: Alright, let's calm ourselves with a few deep breaths. [She asks them to remain silent for a full minute before she resumes.] Okay. We have failed. Our systems keep crashing, and we can't keep them running. Our key stakeholders are frustrated with us for letting them down. Let yourself feel the embarrassment of facing them. Feel the shame and guilt as they overtake your body. [Francois asks for another pause. A minute later she continues.] Now think of the satisfaction we feel when we keep our systems running like clockwork. Imagine our stakeholders smiling and thanking us. Feel the pride and satisfaction of a job well done.

Francois then leads the team through a few iterations, coaching them back and forth from the negative to the positive, ending with the positive.

This technique helps the team realize they can handle the pain of failure and thus relinquish their fear of defeat. It also teaches them how to shift into the positive emotional state needed for peak performance, as discussed in the previous chapter. Francois's team cannot prevent the systems from crashing, but it can use this technique to keep from getting emotionally hijacked when and if the system does go down.

USING A FEAR RELEASE GUIDE TO REDUCE FEAR AND NEGATIVITY

You can use the Fear Release Guide to help you select the most effective techniques for reducing fear and negativity in your team. If you want to dissipate strong and debilitating fear, you'll get the best results with a technique that ranks high in Effectiveness of Fear Reduction. If you need to reduce the fear immediately, use a technique that rates low in the Length of Time Required. The Level of Emotional Trust Required indicates the amount of trust and comfort that must already exist in the team for the technique to prove most effective.

	Fear Release Guide		
Technique	**Effectiveness of Fear Reduction**	**Length Time Required**	**Level of Emotional Trust Required**
Acknowledge the Threat	Medium	Low	Medium
Tell Me Where It Hurts	High	High	High
Accentuate the Positive	High	High	Medium
Occupy the Brain	Low	Low	Low
Desensitize to Fear	High	Low	High
Get Real	Medium	High	Low
Bounce Back	High	High	High

These techniques work for both individuals and teams. In the story at the beginning of this chapter, I used the Desensitize to Fear and Bounce Back techniques when I was dealing with the pain of losing key employees. While Desensitize to Fear helped me handle that difficult period, Bounce Back enabled me to move forward with greater strength to handle similar situations in the future.

These techniques work equally well for groups. However, you want to make sure that you have established the right amount of emotional trust in the team. For the techniques that require high levels of trust, team members must feel comfortable sharing their emotions with teammates and should trust the team leader to guide them through the process in a nonjudgmental and nonembarrassing way. Otherwise, some team members will likely reject the technique or participate only half-heartedly.

In the next chapter, we'll look at how to spread optimal emotions in a team.

CHAPTER 4

Emotional Contagion
Spreading Coherence in a Team

In 1969, two names dominated headlines in the *Los Angeles Times*: UCLA basketball coach John Wooden and cult leader Charles Manson. That year, Wooden took the UCLA Bruins to one of seven consecutive NCAA basketball championships, a feat no other team may ever match. That same year, Manson ordered his followers to murder actress Sharon Tate and seven other innocent people "as gruesomely as possible."

Why would I put the names of two such totally different leaders in the same sentence, one a model of coaching excellence, the other an insane killer? Both men inspired a group of people to do something extraordinary. Both understood how both positive and negative emotions spread instantly among people in close proximity, independent of words and actions. They knew that the most emotionally active person in a group transmits their emotions to the others, who quite often do not realize they have fallen under the spell.

You may never have the chance to work with a team leader as brilliantly motivating as John Wooden, and you hope never to have to work with a leader as diabolical and toxic as Charles Manson. But you will always need to deal with a wide range of emotions, both energizing and toxic, in your team. While you cannot eradicate the negative ones, such as anxiety, jealousy, fear, and anger, from people's minds, you can learn how to keep them from overtaking your team and thwarting its potential.

In this chapter, we'll look at how all kinds of emotions spread among team members and how you can ensure that the most beneficial ones cast a spell on your team.

SPAWNING GOOD CHEER

Former Southwest Airlines CEO Herb Kelleher would frequently stroll down the corridors of Love Field in Dallas, the airline's hub, greeting customers and employees. He always displayed a beaming smile as he happily chatted with everyone in sight. He even hugged some of the employees. As he went from person to person, he literally left a trail of uplifted moods in his wake. After an impromptu visit from their boss, energized Southwest employees felt they could handle any challenges that came their way.

Herb Kelleher could light up peoples' faces, make them laugh, and inspire them to feel part of one big happy family.[1] Even if you lack the charisma of a Herb Kelleher, you too can lighten the mood of everyone around you.

Dispense Optimal Emotions

Lifting the mood of your teammates depends less on *what* you say than on how you *feel* when you say it. Take team leader Janice, who wants to cheer up her team at Gizmodec's as they begin another arduous week on Monday morning. Before she meets with them, she racks her brain to find the right words to stress the importance of their work and what they can bring to Gizmodec's customers. In truth, however, she'll make a stronger positive impact on them if she focuses on feeling her most enthusiastic, maintaining genuinely high spirits, and then explains how to use the new purchase order form (or any other mundane subject). When we're energizing our team, the emotions we radiate matter even more than the words we use.

In 1997, William Doherty, professor of psychology at the University of Hawaii, published research in the *Journal of Nonverbal Behavior* that demonstrates this point. Psychologists have known for some time that a person's mood influences their evaluations of other people and objects.[2] Doherty's experiment used this fact. How, he wondered, would exposure to an emotional person affect someone's evaluation of a series of photographs? To answer this question, he first created three videos in which a woman provided instructions on doing the photo evaluations. In the first video, she clearly displayed a neutral mood. Prior to making the next two videos, Doherty subjected her to hypnotic suggestions that she feel sad in one and happy in the other. The three videos contained exactly the same content and differed only in terms of the emotions of the speaker. Her emotional expressions fell well within the normal range of business conversation.

The subjects who evaluated the photos came to the lab twice, with a three-week interval between visits. On the first visit, they viewed the emotionally neutral video and then rated ten photographs from a cross-cultural photo journal. During the second visit, the researchers randomly assigned the subjects to view either the sad or happy video. After viewing the videos, the subjects again rated the same ten photos.

Doherty found that the ratings reflected significant biases based on the speaker's mood. People who viewed the sad video rated the photographs substantially more negatively than those who viewed the happy version. Furthermore, the subjects who watched the sad video rated the photographs significantly more negatively than they had during their first visit. The opposite happened with those who viewed the happy video.[3]

If people readily catch the emotions of a stranger in a four-minute video, imagine how easily they get infected by a teammate's or team leader's emotions, irrespective of *what* they are saying. Sure, Janice knows better than to complain to her team about this morning's argument with the CFO about her team's budget because she knows that will make them unhappy. But if she shows up at the team meeting feeling stressed out or angry, her mood will bring down the whole crew, even if she's talking about how much Gizmodec's customers love the new software they rolled out last month. It's like walking into the office with the flu; pretty soon everyone's sneezing.

You must assume responsibility for instilling optimal emotions in your team. Make sure that you're truly feeling those optimal emotions before you stroll into the office or convene a team meeting. You set the emotional tone, and false displays will adversely affect people just as much as negative ones. Given the contagious nature of emotions, you want to be a genuine Jolly Janice because a Jaundiced Janice will infect everyone on the team.

Beware of Passing Around Your Bad Mood

We saw in Chapter 2 that a sour facial expression can cause you to feel sour. It can also spread like the plague. In 1995, the *Scandinavian Journal of Psychology* published research conducted by Lars-Olov Lundqvist, a professor and researcher at Orebro University, showing how people rapidly and automatically emulate the facial expressions of others. The researchers placed an electromyograph, which measures the movement of facial muscles, on the faces of subjects while they studied photographs of people who displayed happy, sad, angry, fearful, surprised, or disgusted facial expressions. Lundqvist found that the subjects' facial muscles spontaneously moved to mimic the expressions they saw in the photographs. When participants looked at happy faces, they unwittingly increased muscular activity over the cheek muscle region (mimicking the smile). When they viewed angry facial expressions, they instinctively moved the muscles over their eyebrows (mimicking the anger).[4]

According to John Cacioppo, professor of psychology at the University of Chicago and coauthor of *Emotional Contagion*, the mimicking goes well beyond our facial expressions. During conversation, we also unconsciously mimic the other person's posture, body language, and speech patterns.[5] As your teammates watch and listen to you, they automatically mimic other physiological expressions of emotions, such as rapid eye movements, gestures, and perspiration on your upper lip. In addition, these signals prompt them to feel the way you feel. We will look more deeply into this phenomenon in Chapter 5. This natural human tendency makes your display of emotions one of your most powerful management tools, one you can deploy to evoke optimal emotions in your team. But you can't model genuine positivity and enthusiasm if you're feeling rotten inside. Make it real; never fake it. If Janice still feels angry at the CFO, she should avoid facing the team. Until she can collect herself and brighten her mood, she should send her teammates an email about the happy results of the customer satisfaction survey and postpone the team meeting. That buys her time to use some of the mood-enhancing exercises presented in this book. Even though Janice's voice may tremble for a mere second, and Peter may only briefly mimic it, he will likely feel the accompanying emotions long after the meeting has ended.

When you flash a genuine smile at your team, you want it to work wonders on *all* of your teammates. Given all the cultural differences in today's workplace, you may wonder whether you can actually do that. Do Raul from Brazil and Mahesh from India experience smiles the same way California-born Peter and Valerie do? Paul Ekman, whom we met in Chapter 2, set out to answer this question in 1965.

Ekman originally thought that children learned how to make appropriate emotional facial expressions by observing adults. If environmental factors rather than human genetics produced smiles, then smiles would vary from culture to culture. To verify this hunch, Ekman simply showed pictures of facial expressions to people in the United States, Japan, Argentina, Chile, and Brazil, asking them to describe how the people in the photographs were feeling. People from all of these cultures consistently judged the expressions in the same way. But that did not convince Ekman. What if all of these people had learned facial expressions by watching globally popular movie stars or political figures?

To test this theory, Ekman sought out people who lived in isolated regions and had never seen such international favorites as Jerry Lewis, John F. Kennedy, *The New York Times*, and *Life* magazine. He ended up selecting subjects who inhabited the remote highlands of Papua New Guinea. When Ekman showed these people photographs of faces exhibiting various expressions, he found, to his surprise, that they interpreted them exactly the way a Westerner would. A sad face, for instance, made them wonder whether the person's child had died.

It turns out that a smile is a smile whether you live in Manhattan or Papua New Guinea. Researchers have confirmed that people's facial expressions for at least seven emotions (anger, fear, sadness, disgust, surprise, contempt, and happiness) look the same around the world.[6] Inasmuch as smiles and frowns are primal products of human genetics and evolution, you can rest assured that your smile will positively influence everyone on your team.

Emulate to Communicate

Why do we so quickly mimic the facial expressions and emotional moods of those around us? In an article in the September 2008 issue of *Harvard Business Review*, emotional intelligence guru Daniel Goleman argues that such mimicry and therefore emotional contagion may arise from the mirror neurons in the brain.

Neurons are the core components of the nervous system. When they receive signals from the brain, they cause muscles to contract. You decide to raise your hand to get the speaker's attention during a presentation, and a neuron fires in your brain, sending a signal that tells the muscles in your arm to respond.

According to Goleman, Italian neuroscientists discovered mirror neurons by accident while monitoring a particular neuron in a monkey's brain that fired only when the monkey raised its arm. When a lab assistant casually lifted an ice cream cone to his own mouth, the gesture triggered a reaction in the monkey's neuron. This suggested that the brain is peppered with neurons that mimic, or mirror, what someone else does.

This previously unknown class of brain cells functions as a social antenna, detecting the emotions of others through their actions and then reproducing them in observers. When we're collaborating with our teammates, these neurons create an instant sense of shared experience.[7] They prompt people in groups not only to exhibit one another's facial expressions but also to adopt one another's posture, body language, and speech rhythms. When Peter charges into Janice's office, anger written all over his face and intent on arguing about a major project issue, he immediately and unconsciously emulates her calm composure. He automatically sits down, relaxes back in the chair, stops waving his arms, and lowers his voice. Now they can really communicate and solve the problem. Teams that work closely together mirror each other in many, many ways. That mirroring helps them converge, connect, and communicate more effectively.[8]

Mirroring enables a sense of kinship and support. As Janice's team emulates her broad smile and rapid speech pattern when she talks enthusiastically about resolving a pressing customer issue, they share her excitement. When Peter, feeling pretty beaten-up and defeated, tells the team about an irate customer who would not listen to his offer to replace defective software, the team's mirror neurons help them feel his pain and work hard to help him solve the problem.

Familiarity breeds camaraderie. The more your teammates hear one another's voices and see one another's faces, the more they will converge emotionally and work in synch. As the team leader, you need to get your people together a lot, in person, via videoconference, or in any other way that allows them to see and hear and feel one another's presence. But you must also take an active role in shaping the end result. Use your own emotional influence to help them become a tightly knit unit full of creative potential, rather than a destructive angry mob. Smile easily, play boisterously, and laugh readily. Let your team's mirror neurons spread optimal emotions.

Share Negative News in a Positive Way

Few events in organizational life ignite more emotion than the performance appraisal. A team member's experience during an annual one-hour performance review can influence his or her mood for the rest of the year. Of course, the content of the appraisal makes a big difference. Who wouldn't feel pleased with a highly positive review? And who wouldn't suffer self-doubt and anxiety over a highly critical one? But, as we've seen, content isn't everything. The emotions with which the reviewer delivers the news can play an even bigger role in how it affects the recipient. Peter will respond better to bad news from Janice if she conveys it in an upbeat, positive way.

In Goleman's *Harvard Business Review* article discussed earlier, the author describes research conducted to determine the influence of a boss's emotions during performance appraisals. The study separated employees into two groups. People in one group received a poor performance review from a good-natured boss, who smiled and nodded a lot. People in the other group got a good performance review delivered by an unpleasant boss who frequently frowned and displayed consistently negative emotions. In subsequent interviews the researchers conducted to compare the emotional states of the two groups, they found that employees who had received positive feedback accompanied by negative emotional signals reported feeling worse about their performance than did those who had received cheerful negative feedback. The delivery mattered more than the message itself.[9]

If Janice wants to help Peter reach his full potential, she should insist on top-notch performance, but she should always discuss any shortcomings in a cheerful manner. She may need to tell him, "Thirty percent of your clients have rated your care below our standard," but if she focuses on the fact that she wants to help him to become a stronger member of the team, doing so will help her deliver the message in a genuinely upbeat manner. Never forget that you can't just *tell* someone what you think of their performance, you must *show* your appreciation and support with positive facial expressions and body language.

BECOMING THE TRUE LEADER

When Elaine Hatfield, professor of psychology at the University of Hawaii, first started out as a psychotherapist, she noticed something strange after concluding certain counseling sessions. After working with a seemingly cheerful patient, Hatfield would feel depressed once the patient left. Another patient, who on the surface seemed very nice and relaxed, made Hatfield feel uncharacteristically shy. At the same time, she noticed similarly odd experiences with colleagues. When she talked with an arrogant, competitive professor, for instance, she always felt as if she'd said something stupid when in fact she had not. During one of these uncomfortable exchanges, she saw brief expressions of anxiety on her colleague's face and detected a slight quiver in his voice. That's when it dawned on her that she was catching what others were feeling, despite outward appearances to the contrary.[10]

People can remain so oblivious to the emotions running rampant in their team that they do not realize what's happening. One of Janice's teammates, Stuart, seems supremely calm and professional on the surface, but she finds herself feeling unaccountably angry during a one-on-one conference with him. After a team meeting in which Stuart talks at length about an issue, she also notices the rest of the team bickering on the way back to their cubicles. Professor Hatfield might explain that those feelings arise because deep inside and almost undetectably to others, Stuart actually seethes with unexpressed anger. People can try to bury their true emotions, but they will seep out and affect the people around them in ways they don't really comprehend. As a team leader, you need to make sure that positive, not negative, ones rule the workplace. You can most effectively do that by becoming the source of any emotional contagion, thereby reducing the chances that Stuart's suppressed anger will infect your team.

Realize What Hit You

When you suddenly find that your emotions have shifted for no discernible reason, chances are you caught someone else's suppressed emotions. You can most effectively deal with such a situation if you understand some basic principles of emotional contagion.

In the January 2000 issue of *Psychological Science*, Ulf Dimberg, Monika Thunberg, and Kurt Elmehed published research that shed some light on the phenomenon. When they showed images of happy or angry faces to subjects for only 30 milliseconds and then immediately showed them faces with neutral expression, even though the subjects could not recall the initial photos, they responded with the distinctive facial muscle reactions that corresponded to the happy or angry faces. As you might expect, their facial expressions prompted corresponding mood changes. The researchers concluded that subtle signals could evoke unconscious positive and negative emotional reactions.[11] When Janice or the team meets with Stuart, anyone can catch his anger even if it bubbles to the surface for only the few milliseconds when he can't keep it out of sight.

To make matters worse, Stuart's anger can influence his teammates' emotions even if he sits quietly in the corner and no one even glances his way during the entire meeting. In another *Harvard Business Review* article published in 2001, Daniel Goleman reports that people transmit invisible signals that can alter the mood of others. Yes, you can change the mood of others without saying or doing anything! According to Goleman, psychologists have found that three strangers sitting in silent close proximity will feel the effects of the most emotionally active member of the group within only a minute or two. Similarly, research has found that any group of people meeting together will end up sharing the same mood.[12] If Stuart is the most emotionally active person in a team meeting, everyone else can be infected without having any idea what hit them.

The Institue of HeartMath has found that we all share emotions through the powerful electromagnetic field emitted by our hearts. As we saw in Chapter 1, our hearts' field changes depending on our emotional state. But it might surprise you to learn that your heart's field extends beyond your body to the outside world, radiating from your heart, through your tissues, and into the fields of others. HeartMath researchers have used sensitive magnetometers to establish that this field exists as far as ten feet away from the body. Stuart's field can reach Janet from across the desk, and vice versa. Your nervous system acts as an antenna that can pick up the electromagnetic heart fields transmitted by those around you. It may seem strange, but we automatically and unconsciously sense the heart fields of other people. HeartMath has shown that the signals transmitted by one person's heart can automatically alter the mood-generating physiology of another person, including their hormone levels and cardiovascular functions.[13] This energetic emanation via heart fields provides a plausible explanation for how Stuart's emotions can infiltrate Janice's body and influence her mood, even as he sits silently just a few feet behind her.

Unfortunately, people catch negative emotions much more easily than they do positive ones. According to Cacioppo, when good and bad emotions collide, the bad triumphs.[14] So even if Janice is feeling perfectly peachy, chances are Stuart's subtle signals of anger will bring her (and the team) down.

Dominate the Emotional Field

You can ensure that optimal, rather than detrimental, emotions are spread throughout your team by intentionally making your emotions both optimal *and* highly contagious. Because the person with the strongest emotions automatically propagates them in others, you want to master the art of amplifying your optimal emotions. Make them strong enough to overpower Stuart's restrained anger or any other negative emotions that team members may be feeling.

Exercise some caution, however. Becoming the most emotionally active person on a team doesn't mean you jump up and down like an overenergized cheerleader. Instead, you should make sure you're *feeling* your emotions more strongly than anyone else. There's a huge difference between exuberant exhibitions and deep feelings. I remember working at a company where a fellow named Eric was promoted to CEO. When he called the company's 20 officers together for our first meeting under his leadership, he stood at the podium, speaking passionately about our bright future as he waved his arms and shouted with gusto, "We will blast revenue and profits through the roof!" and "We will turn our competition into roadkill!" The stage shook when he pounded his fist on the podium. At one point he even led the team in a loud chant. "We are winners! We are winners! We are winners!" I've got to say, this display made all of us feel uncomfortable and a little embarrassed. Rather than rousing us with his enthusiasm, he turned us off with a display that we found ridiculous.

Why did Eric's cheerleading fail to inspire us? His antics didn't seem genuine. We felt as if we were watching a cheerleader at a high school football game who doesn't care much about the team on the field but just wants to gain the admiration of the crowd. All of his fist pumping and acrobatic gyrations made him appear like a character performing for the audience. Instead of trying hard to *display* your emotions, focus on truly *feeling* them. Then you can exhibit them in a way people find authentic and compelling.

No emotional state is more contagious than coherence. You will recall from Chapter 1 that coherence occurs when you're experiencing intense heartfelt emotions, and they influence people more than any other emotions in the room. The performing mascot or cheerleader projects an *external* and highly organized display that may or may not reflect heartfelt feelings. The authentic and compelling leader develops the *internal* coherent heart waves that synchronize the parts of the leader's brain and most powerfully influence the emotions and brain rhythms of others. You will recall that coherent waves flow with high peaks and low valleys and, like towering ocean waves, pack the biggest emotional punch. When you attain a state of coherence, you transmit emotions powerful enough to overtake any others that have cast their spell on your team.[15] This occurs no matter how you outwardly *display* your emotions. We did not believe Eric genuinely put his heart into his speech but just went through the motions he thought would make him look like a persuasive leader. If he had achieved coherence, we would have felt it, and he would have gotten us much more enthusiastic about going out there and accomplishing the mission.

When you achieve a state of authentic coherence, don't try to inhibit your emotional display. Let your feelings shine. Traditionally, when we say someone looks "emotional," we don't mean that as a compliment, especially in the workplace. But when your emotions authentically come from your heart, you will impress people with the fact that you feel energized and centered and fully aware. Coherence may prompt you to grin, release the tension in your shoulders, and speak in an engaging tone of voice, perhaps even pounding the table to drive home a point. When you "wear your (coherent) heart on your sleeve," you put your best self forward. Everyone around you will respond by taking you and your words to heart.

Once you get your team into a state of coherence, you will see that it proliferates rapidly. In a study of 46 social groups, HeartMath found that individual coherence reinforces group coherence, and vice versa. Janice's highly positive and supporting mood makes the group happier; the group's happiness makes Janice happier. And so the circle grows.[16]

The lead guitar sets the tone for the whole band. Be the lead guitar, whether you find yourself leading the team or have just joined it as its newest member. When you strike the notes, the rest of the band will jump in and play in harmony.

Broadcast Coherence

As a team leader, you understand the importance of supporting your people. You give them the resources they need, defend them from unwarranted criticism, and show them your deep appreciation. You may even provide emotional support during personal crises. But, even more importantly, you burnish their stars and make them shine as brightly as possible. You motivate them to reach their highest potential as innovators and creative problem solvers. You can find no better way to do that than by helping them feel more coherent, even if they do not suspect that's what you're doing.

Let's say your team faces a huge challenge, such as figuring out how to replace a 30-year-old software application on which your entire company depends. The tentacles of this outdated octopus reach into every company process and every piece of important data and software. Any disruption or failure could cause a total meltdown. You've assigned a brilliant software architect named Sean to lead the effort to untangle the mess that the octopus has made by extracting and replacing the ancient software. He's bright, but he needs to shine at a million kilowatts if he's going to conquer this particular challenge. What can you do to make that happen?

In 2010, Steven Morris published research in the July/August issue of *Alternative Therapies*, showing how one person (the "sender") can facilitate higher levels of coherence in another person (the "recipient"). In Morris's experiments, the senders first got into a state of coherence and then intentionally directed compassion-infused attention toward the recipients without the recipients knowing what the senders were doing. When the researchers conducted many trials with many different participants, using sensors to measure everyone's coherence, they found that senders proficient at achieving high levels of coherence in themselves more successfully increased the recipients' levels of coherence.

Back to you and Sean. You can apply a technique based on this idea to help Sean reach a million kilowatts. First, you must take a few minutes to get coherent using the breathing technique you learned in Chapter 1 and then pay a quick visit to Sean or simply walk with him shoulder-to-shoulder down the hall. You can also use this technique when anything from a false fire alarm to a death in the family emotionally hijacks anyone on your team. If a heated argument over the best way to exterminate a bug in the new software sidetracks Sean, evoke a state of coherence while you're all sitting in the conference room. That will quickly help him get recentered and thinking straight again.

Steven Morris discovered a higher degree of emotional influence when the sender and recipient shared an interpersonal bond. Without some genuine fondness for one another, the sender could not nearly as easily facilitate coherence in the recipient. If you have never gotten to know Sean at a personal level and truly care about his welfare, you will find it harder to burnish his star. But if you know he dotes on his golden Labrador retriever, love to hear his stories about Fido's antics, and tell him how much you admire his connection to his pet, he will unconsciously respond to your emotional broadcast much more readily than if you never ask him about all that dog hair on his sweater.

Use your heart more than your head. Morris found a stronger effect when senders focused more intently on achieving their own high coherence level than on changing the recipient's level.[17] If you concentrate on increasing Sean's brightness by imposing your own emotional state on him, you may overengage your mind at the expense of your heart. That can create performance anxiety, which actually impedes your ability to increase Sean's coherence. Whatever the situation, make sure you pay close attention to achieving and maintaining a high level of coherence yourself. That will almost automatically increase Sean's coherence. Here's a little trick I find useful. Whenever you wish to convey coherence, take a deep breath while concentrating on your own coherence, then let it out as you imagine you're broadcasting it into the room.

MAKING COHERENCE A COMPETENCY

I once led a large group that consisted of several teams, one of which included Alan, an upbeat, jovial young man who took a true interest in his teammate's feelings. He made a point of getting to know each member of the entire group of about 200 people, routinely mingling with them, checking in to see how they were doing, and generally uplifting everyone's mood. The instant you glimpsed him coming down the hall flashing his broad genuine smile, you suddenly felt more upbeat. We loved working in his presence, though I must admit that at the time I did not realize just how huge a contribution he was making to our group's success.

I found out the hard way when our company hit some financial hard times that forced a round of layoffs. Alan received one of the first pink slips. Because many others with greater seniority and more experience could easily do his "real" job in software version control, his manager kept the veterans and let the rookie go. As leader of the larger group, I agreed with this move. It seemed like the right decision at the time, but, boy, were we wrong.

Alan did not just walk out the door with his quick mind and capable hands; he took a big piece of our organization's heart. We felt it immediately. The energy in the group waned and never really recovered. We had always impressed our customers with innovative web applications and process optimization modules. Now, in his absence, we found ourselves losing our zip and never again so totally delighting our customers. It had never occurred to us to persuade our human resources department that we should keep a greater heart and instead let a wiser brain depart.

To prevent this kind of mistake, leaders need to value the emotional coherence of their people as highly as they do their technical or analytical skills. We should consider it as much a competency as any other communication or interpersonal skill and make hiring, firing, and promotion decisions based on it. Myself, I always include considerations of heart in every interview with an applicant and in every performance appraisal of a member of my team.

Hire for the Hot Skill

Why do most companies make hiring decisions based on a candidate's technical, analytical, and interpersonal skills but pay little or no attention to that person's emotional disposition? Because we assume that we need someone on our team who knows how to do the job brilliantly and that we can put up with a lot of grouchiness as long as she gets the results we need. So what if she's grouchy or gloomy all the time? Though I shy away from black-and-white rules when it comes to the messy world of emotions, I've learned over the years to consider optimal emotional disposition a valuable competency. Coherence, in the long run, may matter more than the technical skills a candidate brings to the position. I'd tend to take a habitually coherent Alan over a technically savvy but perennially grumpy Stuart.

Bottom line: It may be easier to train for technical competence than for emotional competence. Sometimes a person has a so deeply ingrained negative emotional state that it just takes way too much time and energy to attempt to change it. You know the story of the scorpion and the frog that needed to cross the river. Though the scorpion scoffed at the idea that he would sting the frog halfway across because he would drown as well, he drove home the stinger any way, explaining, "It's my nature." How, then, do you select candidates who won't sting their teammates with bad attitudes?

First, add coherence to your job descriptions. You don't have to say something odd like "Candidate must be happy all the time"; you can say something like "Candidate must demonstrate the ability to act as a positive force in a team, promoting high energy and a can-do attitude in challenging situations." This sort of description will separate the Alans from the Stuarts. Alan will respond warmly to that idea, and Stuart might deselect himself even before he interviews for the job.

Once you've specified the emotional disposition you prefer, design interview questions that strike to the heart of the matter. For example, you might try these:

Question	Desired Elements in the Candidate's Response
"Can you describe how you have contributed to a team's high energy in the past?"	• Recognition that emotions and energy influence team performance

(continues on next page)

	• Proof of a generally positive and upbeat nature
"Have you or a teammate ever hurt a team's performance with a poor attitude or low energy?"	• Understanding that anyone can display both positive and negative emotions • Evidence that they learned from the incident
"Can you recall a time when you took steps to increase energy or improve a negative attitude in yourself or a teammate?"	• Indication that they know and have used techniques to shape emotions • Assurance that they would take initiative to influence their own and their teammates' emotions

These types of questions will elicit answers that tell you a lot about the candidate's understanding of the role emotions play in the workplace. Choose the ones who express not only knowledge of that fact but whose faces light up when they talk about it.

Formalize Coherence as a Skill

When you turn a particular skill into a formal competency, that skill immediately gains clout. Just giving that designation builds it into HR's formal structure for hiring, coaching, and developing people, and it encourages leaders to weigh it when deciding which individuals they should assign to a project, groom for advancement, or promote. In the case of emotional coherence, the company that makes it a competency will far more likely spend money on training provided by an organization like HeartMath LLC or on exercises conducted by a music therapist. It may even set up a formal mentoring program.

When defining coherence as a formal competency, clarify the specific set of skills, knowledge, and characteristics it entails, using clear, concise, and concrete definitions and descriptions. Your definition might include the traits listed in The Emotional Coherence Ladder that follows. It's not so easy to make a "soft" skill concrete and tangible, but it's absolutely essential. When you do that, you can much more easily include and measure the skill in routine management and performance appraisals. Team members can understand the competency and work to develop it with a personal improvement program or select training options that will address any need for improvement. After completing the emotionally repressed Stuart's performance review, Janice may suggest that he take a HeartMath course and learn to use a biofeedback device. The emotionally competent Alan may, all on his own, look for more advanced training in the art of coherence.

The Emotional Coherence Ladder provides a sample structure that you can use to determine and develop an individual's ability to achieve emotional coherence and spread it throughout a team. Keep emotional contagion in mind at all times. Your ability to spread optimal emotions in your team depends heavily on your own personal coherence.

The Emotional Coherence Ladder		
Level	**Personal Characteristics**	**Typical Shaping Actions**
1. Novice	Gets along well with others and empathizes with the emotions of teammates.	Uses emotional shaping techniques when prompted by someone else.
2. Experienced Beginner	Understands the potentially powerful influence of emotions and shows genuine concern for the emotional well-being of teammates.	Occasionally suggests that the team use a shaping technique.

(continues on next page)

3.	Practitioner	Periodically brings his awareness to his own and the team's emotional state.	Recognizes when an individual or team could benefit from a shaping technique and knows how to apply a number of techniques successfully.
4.	Knowledgeable Practitioner	Maintains awareness of her own and her team's emotional state.	Proactively shapes her own and others' emotions with a wide range of techniques.
5.	Expert	Actively modulates his own emotional disposition to achieve and sustain genuinely optimal emotions and immediately detects the need to shift a team's emotions.	Knows all of the best techniques to use in a given situation and consistently applies the right one with great skill.

Alan can see that he falls into the Practitioner category, but now, with the full model in mind, he can consciously work toward the Expert level. Stuart, with his scant self-awareness and little skill at achieving or spreading coherence, needs help getting onto the first rung of the ladder as a Novice. The model might convince him to aim for that level, or it might send him packing.

No organization needs everyone to become an Expert in emotional coherence. A project manager, a group vice president, and a CEO need to operate at that level, but a computer programmer who spends a lot of time alone and interacts with people only occasionally can get by as an Experienced Beginner or Novice. Herb Kelleher was an Expert in emotional coherence, consistently displaying his ability to influence huge numbers of people. Southwest Airlines needed that from him. On the other hand, Michael, the developmental editor working with me and my publisher on this book, needs no more than a Novice's skill because the three of us never meet face to face and interact only by phone and email. None of us on the team needs more from him.

As with many soft skills, individuals may bring little competency to the party. But once the party starts, you need to think about and talk about and work on it all the time. Show people the competency ladder, and get them climbing higher and higher. Alan brings a knack for emotional coherence to the team, but he can always reach a higher level. Talk with him about his desire to become a team leader himself, share your experiences with building high-energy teams, and encourage him to read books on the subject and attend training programs. As for Stuart, Alan may take him under his wing and help him get at least a rung or two up the ladder. As with any of life's great skills, it's a never-ending journey. Just when you think you've seen and done it all, a big surprise pops out of the bushes, prompting you to do even more to sharpen your skill set.

USING THE EMOTIONAL CONTAGION DO'S AND DON'TS TO SPREAD OPTIMAL EMOTIONS

You can spread optimal emotion in a team more easily than you might think, provided you keep your own optimal emotions running at a high level. These tips can help you do that:

Do	Don't
Focus on feeling your message as much as speaking it.	Inhibit your expression of emotions.
Interact with your team when you're feeling upbeat and positive.	Confront your team when your energy tank runs out of gas or you're feeling downright miserable.

(continues on next page)

Amp up your positive feelings.	Jump up and down like a cheerleader.
Make yourself the source of optimal emotions.	Get infected by someone else's detrimental emotions.
Actively feel and spread coherence.	Leave your team's emotions to chance.
Make coherence a competency.	Hope people will magically develop coherence skills.

CHAPTER 5

The Sixth Sense
Detecting Emotions

A number of years ago, I interned at a software company before gradu-
ating from college. Thrilled at this chance to learn on the job, I could
not believe my good luck when, on my first day, the HR manager said,
"Three teams want you to join them, and you can pick the one you like
best. After you meet with each one, just let me know your choice."

I eagerly walked into a small conference room to meet Team 1, but
even before they began talking, I noticed that I somehow felt a little
dull and sluggish, like I needed a nap. As the team discussed an agenda
item, they sounded like they needed a nap too. What a lifeless group!

When I strolled into the second room, I interrupted a discussion of
Team 2's current project. As they paused to explain their project and
roles with great gusto, I began to feel a little anxious and stressed, the
same way I felt before a big exam for which I hadn't studied enough.
This team seemed almost too lively, as if they were masking some deep-
seated anxiety.

Feeling like Goldilocks looking for just the right fit, I cautiously
entered the third room and met Team 3. Imagine my relief when, after

only a few minutes, I sensed this whole team's calm enthusiasm. I felt centered yet vibrant. As they spoke about their project, ideas kept popping into my head about how I could make some small contribution. Goldilocks had found a good fit.

Emotion, unlike cognition, influences the body's entire nervous system, not just the brain. In this chapter, we'll learn to listen to our bodies and consciously detect the emotions of individuals and groups. Then we'll explore how to thrive in a business environment where other people are reading our emotions (and those of our team), consciously or otherwise.

GETTING A FEEL FOR FEELINGS

The Roman general Julius Caesar could sense the ebb and flow of his soldiers' emotions. In 58 BCE, while preparing a force of 25,000 men to battle the Germanic tribes for control of Vesantio, in what has become modern-day France, Caesar sensed fearfulness in many of his men. Following his battle-hardened instincts, he showed up in the most needed areas at exactly the right time, delivering what they most needed from their commander: a little fatherly encouragement here, a reassuring pep talk there, or even an occasional stern command.

A couple of days before the battle, he met with Ariovistus, leader of the Germanic tribes, on a large mound in an open field, each leader surrounded by several hundred cavalry bodyguards. Hoping to avoid a bloody conflict, Caesar tried to persuade Ariovistus to retreat back across the Rhine River. As the two men talked, Caesar could feel his cavalry escorts growing restless and worried that they might draw their swords and prematurely start a fight. He immediately broke off negotiations and left the battlefield.

During the ensuing battle, the troops performed with such courage and mastery that they quickly routed their opponents and drove them back across the Rhine River into their own homeland. That victory rested, first and foremost, on Caesar's ability to sense the emotional states and needs of his troops.[1]

All leaders need to know what's going on emotionally with their teams. Do people feel overwhelmed by major obstacles? Has fear overridden their rational thinking? Are they growing restless? You can't expect them to tell you when they're feeling negative. They might not be able to put their feelings into words, or they may worry that expressing negative emotions will make them seem weak and needy, inviting disapproval or even dismissal. Not to worry, though, because here comes neuroscience to the rescue, with good advice on how to read emotions in a flash. Your readings, like Caesar's, can tell you exactly what kind of help your team needs.

Bump Empathy to the Next Level

Even if your team usually performs flawlessly, you know that circumstances can sometimes send them off the rails. That's when you most need them to tell you how they're feeling about their work and whether they need your help. Take the case of team leader Rich Knight, who leads a software development team of 15 people. Every Monday morning, Rich holds a status meeting to find out whether everybody is on track. This week they're working with an extremely tight schedule that their clients expect them to meet in three weeks. Unbeknownst to Rich, Monte, a skilled programmer in charge of developing a crucial portion of the software, has fallen so far behind schedule he will almost surely miss the upcoming deadline by a mile. Monte, however, has been keeping that fact a secret. He simply cannot bring himself to speak up and admit the problem because he fears his teammates will think him incompetent. Perhaps he can figure out a way to catch up without alarming Rich and the team. Of course, that thinking only makes matters worse. The sooner Rich learns about the problem, the sooner he can clear the obstacles blocking Monte's work or assign someone to lend him a helping hand. If only Rich could borrow some of Caesar's empathic abilities and read Monte's emotions before a bombshell drops on the whole team in three weeks.

As you will recall from Chapter 4, highly contagious emotions can rapidly spread from person to person. That makes emotion reading possible. What if Rich intentionally catches Monte's emotions, enabling him to feel what Monte is feeling even if Monte never utters a word? This would involve Rich taking empathy to a higher level, where he not only understands and sympathizes with Monte's plight but actually *feels* his emotions. In doing so, however, Rich needs to take care that he feels Monte's stress and anxiety without letting those feelings overrun his own emotions and make him feel just as stressed out as his teammate. Fortunately, neuroscience offers some clues about how many of us can learn to do just that.

According to Vittorio Gallese, a professor of human physiology at the University of Parma, Italy, when we observe someone, our neural circuits automatically activate to match those of the person we're observing. Gallese attributes this neural synchronization to the mirror neurons he helped discover and that we discussed briefly in Chapter 4.[2] As team leader Rich studies Monte who is giving his status update, Rich's neural circuits naturally and automatically come into alignment with Monte's. This means that Rich can do more than just listen to Monte's words and observe his body language; he can also detect Monte's emotional state by paying attention to his own feelings as he observes Monte. He can know instantly whether Monte feels confident and assured or fearful and stressed. Those clues can prompt Rich to probe Monte's feelings more deeply, perhaps in a one-on-one session after their meeting.

During Monte's presentation, Rich must pay close attention to Monte, looking for the telltale signals that indicate various emotions— perhaps the raised eyebrows or rapid speech that accompany Monte's comments about the schedule. At the same time, he must consider his own emotional and physical reactions, as he catches Monte's emotions. Does he start breathing faster? Can he feel the muscles in his arms tightening? This sort of deliberate and careful emotional monitoring does not come easily for most of us, partly because we have not learned the art of how to separate emotions that arise in our own neural system from those sparked, at least in part, by the emotions of others. Yet anyone can get much better at detecting the emotions of others by monitoring how his or her own body feels.

Pay Attention to Your Body

According to Robert Levenson, professor of psychology at the University of California at Berkeley, emotions cause changes in the body in order to prepare it to respond efficiently to a stimulus. We all know the story about the slender mother who lifted a Volkswagen off the pavement to free her trapped daughter. We've experienced it ourselves when we find out that we must deliver results far earlier than we had expected. Suddenly our heart beats faster, and our temperature rises. That's our body kicking into high gear to get the job done.

According to Levenson, most of these physiological changes stem from our autonomic nervous system (ANS) as it prepares our body to respond to a stimulus, say a bear scrambling out of the woods. At that moment, we need our bodies to respond effectively, whether we choose to fight, flee, or freeze. The ANS, located in our lower brainstem, is a primal control mechanism that activates automatically, without our conscious awareness. It rapidly organizes our muscles and organs to respond optimally, while we simultaneously feel an attendant emotion. We see the bear, our ANS fires a warning, our body girds for action, and we feel scared out of our wits. It all happens faster than the bear can say, "Grr!" Our boss needs that report in an hour rather than tomorrow afternoon? We respond physically and emotionally faster than she can say, "You're fired!"

Levenson asserts that different emotions create different effects in our ANS. Each distinct emotion, especially a negative one, produces a unique physiological response.[3] If Monte starts feeling hopelessly behind schedule, he begins to perspire. His breathing grows shallow and rapid. If he blames Rich for giving him too much work, his eyes glare and his teeth clench. Later, if he gets his work under control, his body relaxes.

According to Gallese, when Rich observes Monte, his body experiences the same sensations Monte feels, as if Rich had climbed inside Monte's skin.[4] Rich can instantly detect Monte's fear, anger, and resentment.

Peel Away the Façade

Those handy mirror neurons enable Rich to detect Monte's emotions even when Monte appears outwardly serene. Quite likely a veteran software developer like Monte knows from experience which behavioral displays his boss and teammates find acceptable. Over the years, he has learned to hide his worried reactions to problems in the workplace, even when he's freaking out inside. When he adds his two cents to the status report meeting, he says with the coolness of a cucumber, "My work is coming along fine with no major issues." If others cannot see signs of Monte's anxiety, can they nevertheless learn to *feel* them?

In 1998, University of California at Berkeley Professors Jose Soto, Nnamdi Pole, Loren McCarter, and Robert Levenson presented research at the Society for Psychophysiological Research suggesting that you can best detect negative emotion in another person by paying close attention to your own body's sensations while observing that person. In one experiment, the researchers showed participants videotaped conversations of people discussing important marital issues with their spouses. The researchers asked the viewers to identify the spouses' feelings throughout the discussion. To create a benchmark, the researchers had obtained the spouses' descriptions of their own feelings. The researchers also recorded hard data that measured both the spouses' and the viewers' physiological reactions at the time of the original marital discussion and the subsequent viewings, including heart rate, skin conductance, and other general physiological activity.

The researchers found that some people, though not everyone, accurately detected the spouses' emotions. Interestingly, the facial expressions of an empathic viewer mimicked a spouse's expressions only when the spouse displayed positive emotions. When it came to negative emotions, the viewer's face did not reveal those feelings but their physiological reactions did. For both the spouse and the viewer, faces might look calm and collected even though heartbeats were racing and pores were leaking perspiration. The research suggests that our *bodies* can effectively detect the negative emotions of others.

That's good news for Rich. He can rest assured that he can successfully identify Monte's unhappy state by studying his own body's reactions to his teammate. "Uh-oh, I'm listening to Monte calmly talk about the schedule, but I feel my hands getting colder, my breathing accelerating a bit, and my heart beating a little more rapidly. I'd better take him aside after this meeting and find out what is really going on."

Don't think Monte is an exception to the rule. Because society deems strong public emotional displays of negative emotions unacceptable, we learn to hide them. But hiding them does not make them go away, of course. It's the old "laughing on the outside, crying on the inside" trick we all pull. All that crying on the inside seeps out in subtle and not so subtle ways because negative emotions activate much stronger and varied autonomic reactions than positive emotions. Whereas positive emotions relax and calm our bodies, negative emotions jazz them up.[5] Rich can more easily detect Raging Bull Monte than Cool Hand Monte. In either case, Rich must peel away the façade before he can see and feel Monte's true feelings. To do that, he needs to sharpen his sixth sense.

Hone Your Sixth Sense

You no doubt know people who possess an innate ability to sense others' emotions. You also no doubt know people who seem almost oblivious to other people's feelings. According to Levenson, the people who most accurately detect others' emotions tend to experience and show their own emotions quite freely.[6] If Rich plays the stoic, unmoved by joy or sadness or fear, he might lack the context to sense Monte's emotions. He may not feel them in his own body or recognize them when they arise.

To hone your ability to detect others' emotions, remain willing to experience whatever feelings arise, and then pay close attention to how they affect your body. If Rich stops resisting his emotions and becomes more familiar with the sensations of anger and anxiety, he will learn to tell the difference. That will help him detect the feelings of everyone on his team.

Letting yourself feel the emotions of others doesn't mean letting these emotions overwhelm you. That can cause another set of problems as you get swept off your feet by a flood of someone else's feelings. Fortunately, you can learn to sense another's emotions and observe how they affect your body without letting them emotionally hijack you. Gradually, you will become a more skilled emotional diagnostician. Periodically, pretend you are an objective doctor by placing a stethoscope to your chest and taking your emotional temperature. Try to diagnose any symptoms of unusual sensations. What is causing those bodily reactions? Why has your heart begun beating a little faster? Why have you started to perspire or clench your teeth? Then think about the origin of those symptoms. Do they arise from deep within you, or have you caught them from someone else? Do this in the company of your teammates. Scan their faces and bodies. Listen to their tone of voice. Has Rich caught *your* enthusiasm? Have you caught his dismay?

Remember that it can take a lifetime to become a highly skilled emotional diagnostician. Don't keep your schooling to yourself. Let others know what you're doing, and ask them whether you're doing it well. Don't say, "Hey, Monte, you sure got up on the wrong side of the bed today. Snap out of it, we've got work to do." Instead, try, "Am I sensing a little frustration here, Monte? If I'm right, I'd love to talk about it."

Most people can recognize intense emotions when people actively display them, but in business conversations, people tend to control their emotional displays. That makes it all the more important for you learn how to read the subtle cues that signal another person's true inner feelings. The Emotion Identifier outlines some of the most common emotions that occur in the workplace and the physiological and facial clues that usually accompany them.

	Emotion Identifier			
Emotion	**Facial Expression**	**Body Posture**	**Voice Attributes**	**Physiological Symptoms**
Anger	Brows lowered and drawn together; eyes glaring; jaw tightly clenched; lips thinner	Chest out and angled forward; head bowed	Higher pitch; increase in volume; faster rate of speech	Heart rate and breathing more rapid; teeth clenched
Fear and worry	Upper eyelids raised and lower eyelids tensed; brows raised and drawn together; lips stretched back	Shoulders hunched; arms and legs crossed	Faster rate of speech; moderately higher pitch	Hands colder; breathing shallow and more rapid; perspiring; muscles in arms and legs tremble or tighten
Sadness	Corner of the lips down; inner corners of eyebrows angled upwards; vertical wrinkle between the brows; cheeks raised	Head bent down; shoulders hunched; arms at side of trunk	Low rate of speech; lower pitch and volume	Eyelids heavier; back of throat sore; eyes moisten with tears
Contempt	Lip corners tightened and slightly raised	Body weight settled and low	Low pitch; relatively low volume	Raising the chin; slowed breathing
Interest	Upper eyelids raised momentarily	Body trunk open and exposed	Increase in pitch and volume	

Since a person's expressions during conversation seldom last longer than 0.5 to 2.5 seconds, you must pay strict attention to their face, posture, and tone of voice to be attentive. Also, bear in mind that people try to dampen their emotional displays in the office. Make sure you listen to your own body as well. Can you feel the physiological symptoms that tell you that you've caught someone else's emotions?[7]

MAKING YOUR TEAM MORE ATTRACTIVE

Jon, the Vice President of Sales at Chasseures, a shoe manufacturer, needs to globalize the company's customer support. After careful analysis, he decides to outsource the help desk to an international provider. To identify the best company to take on this job, he does some research, looking for a company with a strong reputation and a long history of success. Three companies make the top of his list: A, B, and C.

In order to choose the best option, he invites each candidate company to send over the leadership team that would handle the Chasseures account. During the scheduled four-hour interviews, he expects the teams to talk about their experience, success metrics, processes, and pricing. While all three candidates bring impressive track records to the interviews and pass Jon's probing questions with flying colors, at the end of the week Jon and his boss, Valerie, feel strongly drawn to Company B. It's hard to pinpoint the reasons. On the surface, B offers no customer service elements A and C can't provide, and B's team did not answer the tough questions any more convincingly. It's not B's experience, metrics, processes, and pricing that gives it the edge; it's something less tangible that Jon can only call his "gut feeling." Valerie agrees: "I can't tell you precisely why, but something in my heart tells me to pick B."

Chasseures has installed a carefully structured process for selecting vendors, placing tremendous emphasis on quantifiable criteria that decision makers can capture in huge matrices that will enable objective comparisons of all the options. Before Jon and Valerie share their interview experiences with Chasseures' other decision makers, they fill out the vendor selection matrices. Not surprisingly, they rate Company B higher in almost every category. When they finish the paperwork and review the comparisons, Company B clearly wins the competition for their business. "Thank God for this objective process!" Valerie exclaims. But did they use an objective process? The fact is, no matter how many numbers they count, they will never make a purely objective decision. Nor can you.

Understand How Emotions Affect Decisions About People

Like most of us, Jon and Valerie make decisions based primarily on emotions and then find the facts that will substantiate those decisions. A report published in *Cerebral Cortex* summarized a study led by Antoine Bechara, professor in the Neuroscience Program at the University of Southern California, supporting the notion that people make decisions based primarily on the emotions they associate with the various alternatives. As Jon interacts with teams from companies A, B, and C, he unconsciously imagines how working with them will make him feel. He chooses B because working with those people makes him *feel* the best. He then finds the facts to support his decision.

This occurs because a part of our brain, the ventro medial sector, contains the linkage between scenarios we've previously experienced and the emotions they sparked. When we consider alternatives during decision making, our brain relies on this linkage to help us project how each alternative will make us feel in the future based on how similar situations made us feel in the past. Naturally, we prefer the one that pleased us the most.

As we've seen in earlier chapters, when we interact with people, we automatically and usually unconsciously sense their emotions. People and teams develop unique emotional signatures. Think of a team's emotional signature as its basic "personality," which includes the unique ways it feels. Although emotions and moods can vary over time, an emotional signature reflects the typical feelings of a person or team. Bob's demeanor suggests affability and optimism, while Michael's projects a generally dour and pessimistic attitude. Which will you choose for your team, regardless of how their skills stack up on paper? To answer that question, your ventro medial sector automatically kicks in, telling you that in the past you felt a whole lot better working with the Bobs of this world.[8]

That's exactly what happened to Jon and Valerie. While interacting with the three teams during the interview process, they were unconsciously comparing how working with each of the teams will make them feel. Jon's ventro medial sector reminded him how much he had enjoyed his association with another vendor, Team X. He's feeling the same way now as he listens to Company B make its case. Team X's optimal emotions had made him feel calm and assured and more at ease with daily problems. His stress level had stayed low, his energy had remained high, and he had performed at the top of his game. More importantly, the yearlong project with Team X had concluded with spectacular results. Of course, he will pick Company B. And, of course, Company B's emotional signature colored his "objective" ratings of each candidate.

Enhance Your Team's Emotional Signature

Now suppose you work for B and want to do everything you can to convince Jon and Valerie to pick your company over your competitors. Sure, you will trot out all your metrics, your track record with similar projects, as well as endorsements from other clients. You will make sure you state the best factual case for hiring you. Good for you. But wait a minute. Have you considered that the decision will hinge just as much, if not more so, on your team's emotional signature? What will you do to help Jon and Valerie project optimal images of the way they will feel working with your team over the next year?

When prospective clients and customers sense your team's emotional signature, perhaps unconsciously, they will include their perceptions in their decision-making process, whether they know it or not. This happens in every conceivable setting, from a taco stand on the corner to a global electronics giant in Japan. We always feel drawn to people who make us feel good. Poet Maya Angelou put it beautifully: "People will forget what you said, people will forget what you did, but people will never forget how you made them feel." It follows that your business prospects brighten when you enhance your team's emotional signature.

Let's assume your team puts tremendous effort into designing and delivering high-quality services on time and at a fair price. If you run a small restaurant, you probably know that your success depends on appealing to your customers' five senses. You create an alluring ambience with attractive décor, appealing music, organic cotton napkins, the aroma of freshly baked bread, and a menu that pleases the palette. But what if your servers shuffle around like zombies? All that carefully crafted ambience goes to waste. As the owner, you must not only worry about Café Elite's physical layout; you must make sure you have made your serving team feel good to customers. But you can't tell them to be happy any more than you can tell them not to get the flu. You must provide the leadership that will help them feel truly contented to work at Café Elite and provide five-star service. You might try shaping their emotions at the source with the music and breathing exercises discussed in Chapters 1 and 2.

Emotional signatures do not matter as much on the shop floor in an old-school manufacturing company as they do in a new-school service-based business. If your team makes and sells teddy bears, you focus on the emotional attractiveness of the bears. All successful businesses strive to make their products emotionally attractive to customers because emotional appeal figures so prominently in a customer's buying decision. "Oh, won't that fat fuzzy little critter make Keisha happy! I can't wait to see her cuddling it when I tuck her in at night." On a larger scale, automobile manufacturers go to great lengths to create emotionally appealing vehicles, with sleek body lines, chrome details, plush leather seats, and—oh my—that wonderful new car smell. They build in performance features that tempt buyers' emotions, such as the thrill of pressing the gas pedal and going from 0 to 60 in five seconds. Buying a new car isn't just about reliable transportation; it's even more about how the car makes you feel when you climb behind the wheel.

In the service economy, emotional signature becomes paramount. If Jon were evaluating your team, how would he react to its emotional signature? Suppose you decide you should enhance it. If so, you might introduce more novelty by shifting job responsibilities or encourage the team to take an occasional play break to counteract burnout.

Of course, your team's emotional signature does not just matter to customers, it makes all the difference in the world to people considering whether to join and stay with your team.

Acknowledge What Emotions Can Add to the Facts

When I was a young manager, I remember working for a company where the HR department required that all managers take a training course on how to interview job candidates. The program, called "More Than a Gut Instinct," revolved around the premise that we should trust cold, hard facts over our intuition or gut instinct. In other words, judge candidates based on their answers to questions about how they handled situations and accomplished goals in the past. As Sergeant Joe Friday liked to say on the classic television show, "Just the facts, ma'am."

Certainly a candidate's historical success validates his or her on-the-job effectiveness, but Antoine Bechara's research clearly supports the fact that we cannot fully set aside our emotions when making decisions. If so, then we might as well consider our emotions when making that big decision. Otherwise, struggling to ignore our feelings may stymie the whole decision-making process.

Bechara asserts that people who manage to disengage their emotions when making complex decisions, such as selecting someone who will make an ideal addition to a team, will end up making a shortsighted decision that will prove mistaken in the long run. He bases this conclusion on research conducted with subjects with damaged ventro medial sectors. Without this mechanism that allows them to assess how choosing a particular alternative will make them feel, they find it terribly difficult to make a decision at all. In desperation, they may finally decide, but many of their decisions, while working out fairly well in the short term, prove misguided in the long run. This especially holds true with decisions about complicated business or social matters, when a decision maker cannot precisely calculate future outcomes and must therefore rely on intuition, approximations, hunches, and guesses.[9] If Jon can't engage those good old gut instincts when choosing the best vendor, he will probably dither around for a while and eventually, in frustration, just pick the one that offers the lowest price. As with a new pair of shoes, the cheapest ones will usually fall apart long before a more costly but higher-quality alternative, especially if the better shoes just "feel" right.

Looking back on it, I wish my HR department had offered the opposite course: "How to Use Your Gut Instincts to Make Great Decisions." Then I might have become more adept at how to read emotional signatures much earlier in my career.

ENHANCING INTEGRITY

Former President Bill Clinton knew the power of a good cry. He let his tears flow freely, whether prompted by a tragedy befalling a fellow American or the death of a political ally. In a *New York Times* article in 2010, Jennifer Steinhauer describes how Bill Clinton stopped feeling embarrassed about public crying in the early 1990s, when it helped him win the highest office in the land. Shedding tears made him appear more human to voters.[10] When his wife Hillary won the New Hampshire presidential primary in 2008, President Clinton attributed the win to the fact that "people saw who she was" when she came close to tears after a reporter asked her how she kept going on the rugged campaign trail.[11]

People prefer leaders who are not afraid to reveal their feelings. They just don't trust the stone-faced, ramrod-straight, unsmiling general who never bats an eye when his troops suffer defeat. They want a leader who shares their elation and "feels their pain." This applies to team leaders. If you acknowledge the fact that others can detect your true emotions, consciously or not, you should not try to disown them. Let your people know how you really feel. They won't think you weak; they'll know you share their humanity. That knowledge can only increase your credibility.

Become More Authentic

How often have you feigned contentment while you really felt rotten inside? We all do it. I remember the day my boss called me into his office to tell me he had just received an angry complaint from one of the largest users of our website. While he visibly kept his cool as he explained the customer's concerns, I could tell that the customer's phone call had deeply upset him. After a brief chat, I left his office to deal with the situation, casually saying, "I'm sorry you had to field such an upsetting call first thing Monday morning." He actually snapped at me. "I am not upset!" That reaction dropped my trust in him a few notches. If he couldn't own up to his honest feelings, what else might he be hiding from me?

I suppose the rare individual may *authentically* remain unfazed in the heat of battle, but most people can't. If, like 99 percent of human beings, you can't, then let it out. By now, you should realize that your feelings could easily seep out no matter how hard you try to hide them. Your facial expressions, body language, and other physiological signals will reveal your feelings, whether you like it or not. So you might as well like it.

Strive for congruence between your display of emotion and your true inner feelings. That will build trust with everyone around you, teammates and customers alike. If an incident occurs that makes your emotions flare, let it show. Let's pretend you're the team leader from Company A who wants to persuade Jon to pick you over your rivals. You take great pride in your team's ability to maintain high levels of energy and optimism, but on the way to the interview a delivery truck rear-ends your car. Neither you nor your two colleagues suffer any serious injuries, but you all feel badly shaken up. The sound of the screeching tires and crushing metal and shattering glass still haunts you as you sit down to chat with Jon. Not wanting to get off on the wrong foot, you do not tell John about the car crash. How, then, do you imagine he will react to your nervous energy and distracted demeanor? Chances are he will think the project makes you feel that way, and he's not about to hire someone who does not feel supremely confident about taking it on. Hold out your shaking hand and tell him about the accident, showing him the reason you may seem a little shaky at the moment.

Reduce Emotional Labor

Some companies insist that their employees engage in what sociologist Arlie Hochschild calls "emotional labor." She first defined this term in her book, *The Managed Heart: The Commercialization of Human Feeling*. By it she meant "the management of feeling to create a publicly observable facial and bodily display." Emotional labor occurs when an employee suppresses a negative emotion or evokes a positive emotion to conform to the rules of "feeling" prescribed by their employer. These may appear in formal policies and guidelines, or they may be dictated by the organization's culture. It happens when neurosurgeon Shanti evokes artificial empathy for her surgical patients, when security guard Rick hides his fear while policing a shopping mall where someone reported seeing a man with a gun, and when Keiko slaps on a smile as she takes orders for burgers and fries. It also occurs when policy or the culture demands that employees labor to make other people feel a particular way. Hochschild argues that emotional labor forces people to alter their personality to conform to behavior far different from their usual disposition.

People know emotional labor when they see it. Faking emotions will not end up satisfying the customer or helping you get great results. If Shanti's empathy seems forced, if Rick's face does not portray confidence in the face of danger, and if Keiko's smile doesn't flash her sincere pleasure, patients will seek a new doctor, shoppers will not dive for cover, and hungry customers will walk across the street for a happier meal. Worse, Shanti and Rick and Keiko will feel like con artists and shams. Hochschild points out that over time emotional labor may lead to workers' emotional exhaustion and burnout. As we learned in Chapter 1, emotional dissonance, which occurs when people display emotions that they don't really feel, causes stress because all that effort to suppress true feelings creates enormous internal tension. Acting inauthentic over time may result in feeling detached not only from one's own true feelings but also from other people's feelings as well.[12]

In 2002, an article written by Celeste Brotheridge, a professor in the School of Management at the University of Quebec at Montreal, and Alicia Grandey, an industrial/organizational psychologist in the Department of Psychology at Pennsylvania State University, was published in the *Journal of Vocational Behavior*. According to the article, the more employees faked their emotional expressions at work, the more they also reported distancing themselves from customers and treating them as objects. That spells disaster for anyone working to get results in a service-based economy.

How can you make sure your people genuinely feel the emotions needed for their jobs? It starts with letting Shanti and Rick and Keiko know that you expect them to share their true feelings with teammates and customers. Shanti's patients will trust her more if they know that she takes their condition seriously enough to express her genuine concern for their well-being. Shoppers will trust a frankly worried Rick to protect them from harm. And hungry diners will keep coming back to Keiko with her genuinely infectious smile. This takes us back to the need to shape optimal emotions in the workplace. No, you do not try to teach people how to fake feelings; you do try to help them develop and show their authentic appreciation or even love to their coworkers and customers. Keep in mind that you want people to feel comfortable discovering and displaying their best and truest selves.

According to Brotheridge and Grandey, when employees emote their true feelings, they don't fall victim to the negative effects of emotional labor.[13] The following table will help you learn to spot the differences between fake and authentic emotional displays.

Emotional Labor Versus Emotion Shaping	
Workers are faking it when they:	**Workers are authentic when they:**
Resist expressing their true feelings.	Shift unwanted emotions at their source.
Pretend to have emotions that they don't really have.	Authentically generate positive, coherent emotions.
Hide their true feelings about a situation.	Use coherence-building techniques in the midst of stressful situations.

Know Where to Draw the Line

We've seen that when you're not feeling upbeat and positive, you should own up to and not hide your true emotions. However, you need to know where to draw the line between throwing a tantrum and admitting your anger. Had my boss blown up at me and thrown a paperweight at the wall, I would have distrusted him even more than when he tried to mask his real feelings.

According to a September 12, 2013, blog post on *BBC Capital* by Ron Alsop, a freelance writer and business consultant, attitudes toward emotional expression at work depend on the industry and corporate culture. For instance, creative businesses, such as advertising and publishing, that value individuality, tend to more easily tolerate outbursts of negative emotion. The head of a design studio might get away with shouting and berating people at work, but such displays could cost a Federal Reserve chairman a job. Carefully consider the norms in your industry and company before you fully express your emotions.

Also watch out for double standards. The same blog post proposes that crying can generally make a man seem warmer and more compassionate, enhancing his reputation, while that same display can make a woman appear weak and manipulative.[14]

Such double standards can carry over to other types of emotional displays at work. Victoria Brescoll, assistant professor of organizational behavior at Yale University, and Eric Uhlmann, research fellow in the Ford Center at Northwestern University, reported some revealing results of a study published in *Psychological Science* in 2008. They asked dozens of subjects to view a videotaped job interview in which a man or woman professional described either feeling anger or sadness, and then they invited the subjects to judge each person's competence and status in business. Men who expressed anger generally received higher status marks than men who expressed sadness or no emotion at all. For women, however, expressing anger created the opposite effect. They consistently received a lower status and competency ranking than either angry men or unemotional women. The study went on to propose one crucial technique for ensuring that negative emotional displays enhance rather than harm a woman's (or man's) career.

When a woman displaying negative emotions attributes the emotion to something external, she doesn't suffer a drop in status or competence.[15] So if Company A's team leader Suzanne feels angry over losing the competition for the Chasseures' business, she should go ahead and own up to and express that emotion, but she should also make sure people know she's angry because her team took the interview too lightly and didn't adequately prepare. If Suzanne lets people think she's just upset over losing without attributing it to a specific cause, they might perceive her as an inherently angry person who lacks self-control. Similarly, if Suzanne cries in front of her colleagues, she should specify the reason for her tears, perhaps saying something like, "We may have to lay off some of our people because we couldn't land that contract." That's much better than letting people think she's the kind of gal who always lets her emotions overwhelm her.

Acceptable displays of emotion also vary from country to country. In a blog post on the American Society of Mechanical Engineers' website in March 2011, management consultant and author Carol Goman discusses how the acceptability of emotional displays depends largely on the national culture. She contrasts what she calls *affective cultures,* which approve of emotional displays, from *neutral cultures*, which do not.

This doesn't mean that people in neutral cultures do not possess strong feelings, just that they tend to monitor and dampen intense emotions. Members of an affective culture may find folks from a neutral culture rather cold and aloof, whereas those from a more neutral culture view folks from an affective culture as temperamental hotheads. Observers have found that the Japanese, Indonesians, British, Dutch, and Norwegians disdain intensely emotional reactions, while the Italians, French, Americans, and Southeast Asians find them much more acceptable.[16] You might get away with yelling at an Italian, but in the presence of a Londoner you'd better keep a stiff upper lip.

USING THE EMOTION DETECTOR TO DETECT MOODS AND EMOTIONAL SIGNATURES

Anyone can become more skilled at detecting the emotions of others by paying closer attention to all the signals that alert you to how people are feeling. Try using these four steps in situations where you believe a keener understanding of peoples' emotions will help you lead them more effectively.

Step 1: Get Prepared.

- Become familiar with a neutral facial expression (i.e., no emotions) and a calm body posture, to provide a benchmark for detecting others' emotions.

- Practice becoming acutely aware of how different emotions affect your body, including the feeling of calm.

Step 2: Clear and Focus.

- Become present and fully attentive by taking a few deep breaths and clearing away any negative emotions you're harboring.

- Become attentive to the other person or team, opening yourself to whatever feelings arise.

Step 3: Choose Your Primary Method.

Method	Use When Detecting ...
Facial	An individual in close proximity.
Vocal	An individual who is speaking.
Posture	An individual who is far enough away that you can't see their face or hear their voice.
Physiological	A team when the teammates are convened (or) An individual who displays few emotions.

Step 4: Use the Chosen Method (in conjunction with the Emotion Identifier in the chart on page 101).

Method	To Detect Mood Changes	To Detect Emotional Signatures
Facial	Watch moment-to-moment changes in facial expressions.	Compare facial expressions with a neutral face.
Vocal	Listen for moment-to-moment changes in voice attributes.	N/A

Posture	Pay attention to shifts in body posture.	Compare body postures with a neutral body posture.
Physiological	Sense shifts in physiological symptoms.	Compare physiological symptoms with your emotions when feeling calm.

Note the "N/A" for using vocal clues to detect emotional signatures. No solid neutral benchmark exists for this category because vocal pitch, volume, and rate of speech vary so greatly from person to person. Nevertheless, you can use voice to detect a given individual's changing emotions.

Make becoming an expert emotional detector a lifelong project. You will never become clairvoyant, but you will learn to see and feel emotions that slip past less dedicated emotion detectors.

CHAPTER 6

The Engaged Heart
Connecting to a Deeper Purpose

Sheryl Thomas, leader of the Operations Technology team at North American Trucking, knows how to launch a new project. When her freshly assembled team tackles a project to help drivers load trailers more efficiently, she walks them through all the reasons North American needs optimal solutions. Because she knows that teams with a clear and compelling purpose get the best results, she spends a lot of time at the outset making sure every team member feels the purpose in the very marrow of their bones.

"Why does this project matter?" she asks the team over and over. The team gives her the scripted responses: "More efficiency will enhance the bottom line." . . . "Greater safety will prevent injuries and reduce insurance costs." . . . "Those results will improve our reputation as the most reliable delivery service in the country."

These logical answers make the business case, but one final answer shows that the project has captured the heart of each team member: "Reduced driver stress will make roads safer for families from New York to Portland." That makes Sheryl's own heart sing, "Yay! We got it!"

Some missions, or purposes, satisfy your intellect with their logic, but the most powerful ones touch your heart and literally ignite high energy and enthusiasm.

In this chapter, we'll explore the central role of a compelling purpose in igniting optimal team emotions and performance, as well as examine specific ways you can tap the incredible power of a great purpose to get the sort of results you can't get with cold, hard logic alone.

INSPIRING YOUR TEAM

In 1945, Masura Ibuka cofounded the Tokyo Telecommunications Engineering Corporation (now Sony), amid the ruins and devastation of postwar Japan. The upstart company would pursue the goal of repairing and building electrical equipment, even though it lacked the machinery and scientific equipment to accomplish that goal. Wisely, Ibuka did not sit around worrying about what his company lacked in terms of infrastructure and potential markets but instead focused on defining a compelling purpose for his fledgling enterprise. He went beyond merely answering the question, "What will we do?" He proposed that the company first figure out, "*Why* are we going to do it?"

Ibuka and his partners thoughtfully spelled out their intention that their people "experience the sheer joy that comes from the advancement, application, and innovation of technology that benefits the general public" and that the company must "elevate the Japanese culture and national status." These purposeful words arose from deep inside the company's leaders and reflected their personal passion for inventing new products, honoring their country, and making a difference in the world. Their mission sparked a series of amazing innovations, including the first pocket-sized radio, the first videotape recorder for the home, and the Sony Walkman. These and countless other pioneering achievements sustained Sony's success for decades.[1]

Today, businesspeople do not question the need for a company or team to articulate a clear purpose. Dan Pink, author of several insightful books, including *Drive: The Surprising Truth About What Motivates Us*, has won admiration for his research into the fact that a business's purpose, in the sense of achieving a greater good, can motivate people more effectively than conventional facts and figures and carrots and sticks. Another champion of this approach, Simon Sinek, author of *Start with Why: How Great Leaders Inspire Everyone to Take Action*, delivered a popular Ted Talk in which he extolled the virtue of focusing on the why of a business more than the what. He eloquently asserted that a company's clear and compelling answer to the why question will motivate workers to excel and customers to buy, no matter what products or services are supplied. Both gurus make a strong case for devising a motivating purpose.

Even though we no longer need to question whether a team needs a compelling purpose, we still need to consider what ingredients make the most compelling and powerful purpose. And, once again, neuroscience comes to the rescue with a good answer. Let's look at some recent research that helps explain why Sony's purpose lit a spark that ignited such innovation and global success.

Provide the Spark of Life

Mary-Helen Immordino-Yang, a scientist and researcher at the Brain and Creativity Center at the University of Southern California, says that when people get inspired, they feel more physically alive. In her lab, she recorded images of subjects' brains with a scanner while telling them two different stories. One story made them feel truly inspired, as they confirmed later in interviews; the other interested them but did not inspire them. Immordino-Yang then carefully studied the subjects' brain scans. The inspiring stories, she found, activated the part of the brain, the medulla, that regulates our vital functions, whereas the interesting stories did not light it up at all. Since the medulla controls our breathing, heart rate, and blood pressure, Immordino-Yang's research revealed that the reason we feel so moved by an inspiring purpose is that it activates the same neural systems that keep us alive. Inspired by a great purpose that literally enlivens them, team members maintain optimal emotions and turn in super performances.[2] But what exactly qualifies as an inspiring purpose?

An inspiring purpose drives us to surpass the ordinary, to do more and accomplish more than we ever thought possible. Think about how you feel when you hear a story about someone who did something exemplary. Take Nelson Mandela, who languished in a South African prison for 27 years because the South African government, dominated by the white minority, feared losing power to the black majority. When the government finally released Mandela, instead of seeking revenge for his unjust incarceration, he immediately delivered an inspiring speech in which he declared his commitment to peace and reconciliation with the white minority—an extraordinary gesture of forgiveness.

Even today, thinking about Mandela's response upon his release inspires me to believe that I too can go beyond the ordinary and follow his lead by setting aside my personal concerns for the sake of a greater good. But the effect inhabits not just my mind; it cascades through my whole body as I feel a boost of energy and a distinct throbbing in my heart and upper body. I feel it because Mandela's story stimulates my medulla, which literally lights up my core with an energy that prepares my entire being—mind and body—for taking action.

It all comes down to feelings. The Japanese, physically and emotionally devastated after their World War II defeat, faced the huge challenge of picking up the pieces and restoring the country's economy and national sense of honor. Enter Sony, with its inspiring mission, and suddenly Japanese businesspeople saw and *felt* that they could play a greater role in the recovery than they had ever thought possible. Sony's purpose helped bring a whole country back to life.

Similarly, veteran software developers Sheryl and her team usually kept their noses buried in writing code, but once they understood the implications of their efforts to achieve greater loading efficiency, they rallied around an emotionally satisfying purpose. Because the new software will alleviate the time crunch and reduce weariness and stress for over 10,000 drivers across North America, the team will not only make the drivers' lives easier, they will likely save lives. Less driver exhaustion equals fewer accidents. That purpose brought Sheryl's team to life.

An inspired team develops an expanded sense of their jobs and their vital role in their company's success, and that makes them feel as though they can do anything, even the seemingly impossible. With optimism and high energy pulsing through their bodies, they can conquer the world, but only if you pull them above the realm of mundane thinking.

Add "Extra" to the Ordinary

It takes more than encouraging words to get a team thinking beyond the ordinary. If you ask most people about the purpose of their work, they will often respond with something as blandly straightforward as, "Our purpose is to satisfy our customers." Or they might spout the all-to-familiar corporate refrain, "Our purpose is to maximize shareholder value." On the most mundane level of all, they might say, "Our purpose is to keep our jobs." All of those statements express the worm's-eye view.

To get people to take a satellite's-eye view, you must help them re-define the purpose of their work with broader and more expansive thinking. I often use certain pointed questions to guide a team toward a loftier view of their purpose. Every business unit and team should seek its own answers within the larger corporate context. Note how the purpose-broadening questions I use encourage the team to think of providing value beyond the ordinary.

The Corporate Context

✓ What motivated the company's founders to create this company?

✓ What unique solutions and benefits did they offer their customers?

✓ What excites our customers?

✓ What past, present, and future accomplishments set us apart from our competitors?

✓ What difference has our company made in the world?

✓ What do we want other people to remember about our contributions and accomplishments?

The Team Level

✓ What major contribution can our team make to the company's success?

✓ What do we do that makes our colleagues and customers happy?

✓ What does our work do to give our company a competitive advantage?

✓ What do we do that no one else can do?

✓ What legacy do we want to leave?

✓ What future possibilities excite us?

✓ What difference does our work make in the lives of others?

Remember that the team's purpose needs to tie into the organization's overall purpose. If the leaders of North American Trucking don't care a whit about driver safety, it doesn't make sense for Sheryl's team to define their purpose in those terms. The lack of alignment with the corporate purpose would surely cause a conflict. If Sheryl's team writes software that will dispatch drivers on time so that they don't have to drive too fast to make their schedule, even when that means a shipment doesn't get loaded, the new software will disappoint the company's operations department if their highest priority is making sure all shipments get delivered on time every day. If the new software does not meet the company's objectives, it violates *their* purpose and could easily lead to a disruptive conflict. Make sure your team's purpose is congruent with your company's mission and goals.

As another example, my agent and partner, Michael Snell, began his career in college textbook publishing in the mid-sixties. Jim Leisy, the founder and president of the Wadsworth Publishing Company, won his heart when he said during a recruiting interview, "We do not publish books. We change people's lives by supplying information in book form that will help them live happier and more productive lives." The editorial team thought their work made a big difference in the world. And that principle guides Michael's work to this very day. People who worked for Wadsworth definitely saw the satellite view, which inspired them to do the sort of extraordinary work that made the company a leader in its field.

Of course, once you've defined an inspiring purpose at any level and have enshrined it in a gilt frame on the wall, you'd better live up to it. If you broadcast your purpose as "providing products and services that enhance the lives of the general public," you must invest in the tools and personnel that will deliver on your promise. Otherwise, your soaring mission will quickly crash and burn. Lip service kills inspiration.

Make the Mission Top-of-Mind

For a great purpose to perform its magic, it must be in the forefront of people's consciousness. It can't just occupy a far corner of the mind, where you only access it on special occasions, such as a sales call to a major client or an interview with a reporter. Joseph LeDoux, professor of neuroscience and psychology at New York University, has observed that the human mind can hold only one conscious thought at a time, be it mundane and boring or sublime and emotionally explosive. LeDoux argues, however, that emotional explosions easily blast mundane matters aside. In other words, an inspirational purpose, one that team members feel in the very core of their bodies, easily becomes top-of-mind, a critical prerequisite for innovation.[3]

People come up with their most innovative ideas when they suddenly think of relationships that had never occurred to them before. A Sony engineer, bored to death during a long airplane ride in the late 1970s, wished he could while away the hours listening to his favorite music. That sudden epiphany got him to thinking about how his company could provide a solution. This gave birth to the Sony Walkman. If that fellow had not held Sony's mission in his heart, he probably would not have connected his personal need with a corporate solution. To foster this sort of insightful thinking, you want to make sure your team always keeps the corporate and team purpose firmly in mind. When your team's purpose inspires them, everyone will naturally keep it top-of-mind, where it can spark those Aha! moments that can lead to innovative ways to achieve the mission.

An inspiring, emotionally arousing purpose can also help motivate a team to delve into the nuances and particulars needed to implement an innovation that fulfills the mission. LeDoux points out that when people experience aroused emotions, they pay closer attention to the details.[4] Successful implementation is in the details. Otherwise, even the most creative solution will never see the light of day. In Sony's case, company engineers needed to think through a ton of details about design, parts, manufacturing, performance, quality, marketing and sales, and customer needs. That required a virtual around-the-clock mental immersion in the project. And you know what fueled that immersion: Sony's inspiring mission.

You want your own team to think about their purpose while they're taking a shower, playing tennis, commuting to work, or sitting on the beach looking at a sunset. A weak, vague, or emotionally neutral mission will not do the trick because it will not embed itself deeply enough in their conscious minds to guide their everyday thinking. At the end of this chapter, you'll find some useful tips on making sure your team's purpose strikes just the right emotional chord.

Most importantly, you can keep your team's purpose top-of-mind by fully integrating it into your daily conversation. Print it on the top of all your meeting agendas, ask everyone to offer novel ideas during meetings, visit with them one on one to spark creative thinking, and even emblazon it on a poster. In its heyday, IBM placed THINK signs in every corridor in its plants worldwide, providing a constant visual reminder that the company would financially reward anyone, even a lowly machinist, who came up with an idea that made or saved the company money. Sheryl's team built a cardboard caricature of a uniformed truck driver, complete with a "Dan" name tag, which they installed as a sort of mascot in their team work area. That tangible reminder of their mission kept them constantly focused on making sure Dan returned home safely at the end of a long day.

Satisfy the Craving to Feel

According to Marvin Zuckerman, professor of clinical psychology at the University of Delaware, most people long to feel some degree of emotional sensation. However, that desire varies widely from person to person. High-sensation seekers savor the weekends so that they can go skydiving or speeding along mountain curves on their racing bike. At the other end of the spectrum, low-sensation seekers would rather spend their days off lying in a hammock daydreaming about a leisurely canoe ride on a placid pond. Most of us fall somewhere between the two extremes.[5]

When you find yourself stuck in a boring home life or job, you may find yourself craving something more exciting and will intentionally create intense experiences. At home, Robert, one of Sheryl's teammates, sometimes gets so bored that he watches extremely violent movies, picks a fight with his wife, or gets aggressive on the tennis court. At work, Robert may seek out the latest gossip about his coworkers, incite the team over this year's poor raises and bonuses, or bully Steve, the weakest member of the team. His boredom prompts him to create the missing drama in his life. If it becomes a habit, he may end up in divorce court one day and then lamely explaining to a prospective employer why he got fired from his last job the next. No marriage or team can withstand all that drama for long.

An inspirational purpose can cut down the sort of office commotion that adversely affects productivity. According to an article in the *Review of General Psychology* by Eric Foster, former professor of marketing at the University of Pennsylvania's Wharton School, office drama, such as gossip, satisfies workers' emotions the same way that reading a novel can.[6] If your people can't fulfill their primal craving for emotional stimulation in positive ways, such as pursuing a new project or fulfilling an inspiring purpose, they'll satisfy it in detrimental ways through office drama. Gossiping and unnecessary conflicts not only waste time but also cause a certain amount of emotional damage, and an emotionally damaged team will not perform at the optimal emotional level needed to spark innovation.

You want to make your team's purpose emotionally strong enough to satisfy their craving for emotional sensations and pull them away from destructive office drama. When Robert feels fully engaged with the task of making the highways of North America safer for families, he will less likely waste time on spreading nasty rumors or stirring up conflict. Meaningful work cancels the need for other forms of drama.

RESONATING WITH YOUR PEOPLE

In 1979, Ross Millhiser, vice chairman of Philip Morris, the large tobacco company, said, "I love cigarettes. It's one of the things that makes life really worth living." Millhiser and other company executives maintained an almost defiant attitude toward anyone who suggested that smoking wasn't a good practice. In the middle of a meeting with people who did not work for the company, they would pull out their packs of cigarettes, light up, and throw the packs on the table for all to see. They even pushed cigarettes on their employees, smokers and nonsmokers alike, by giving everyone packs of cigarettes to take home with their paychecks. Even with mounting evidence that smoking causes a host of health problems, including cancer, Philip Morris aggressively marketed their product to women and young people.

The love of cigarettes and the rebellious right to smoke them, no matter what the consequences, formed the core of Philip Morris' purpose and inspired its people to make the company an industry leader.[7] It would not have inspired me, or anyone else opposed to smoking, but it did work for a lot of folks for many decades.

This story illustrates that a purpose that inspires one person may fall flat for another. Given the wide range of differences people bring to their work, you need to figure out what resonates with most of your people most of the time.

Strike a Chord with Life Schemes

According to a 2001 article published in the *Review of General Psychology*, authored by Dan McAdams, professor and chair of the Department of Psychology at Northwestern University, everyone possesses a life scheme that gives them a sense of order and meaning in their life. A life scheme is a cognitive representation of one's life, much like a story. It organizes an individual's perspective on the world, represents that person's personal ideals, and defines the events he or she deems most relevant to those ideals. It embodies a person's basic identity. Individuals feel most inspired by a corporate or team purpose that fits snugly into their life scheme or that motivates them to shift their life scheme to encompass the purpose.[8]

The "smoking is good" purpose matched the life schemes of Ross Millhiser and other Philip Morris executives. Perhaps they grew up watching John Wayne movies and listening to Hank Williams. Whatever their experiences were, they identified at a gut level with the fiercely independent, cowboy image of the Marlboro Man that dominated the company's advertising campaigns. If you worked for the company and related to that image, you resonated with your employer's purpose. If it repelled you, then, of course, you may have looked for a job where the purpose better suited your principles.

When defining an inspiring purpose for your organization or team, be sure to engage all of your key players in the process. Bear in mind that each individual has built a unique life scheme. Don't impose your own preferences, and never assume that one size fits all. Interview people, invite their ideas, and kick around a lot of different ideas. In time, you will discover which goals and missions inspire your team the most.

Also prepare yourself to lose some people with whom a great purpose does not resonate. If a teammate surprises you by saying he finds the idea of working for highway safety ridiculous and can't help but poke fun at such "stupid idealism," you should probably suggest that he find a job where he can more fully relate to the team's purpose. In his landmark book *Built to Last*, business consultant and author Jim Collins proposed that people would eventually leave an organization if they don't align with its ideology. By way of illustration, do you think that the son of a naturopath who grew up eating organic food and married a practitioner of homeopathic medicine would stay at a company like Philip Morris for 25 years? Would the company want him to stay? You can imagine all the conflict that would attend that union of opposites.

Make sure you see a good fit between any prospective teammate's life scheme and your team and company purpose. Share your team's purpose with the candidate. Ask for feedback. Does it inspire them? Or do they smirk a little when you discuss it? Remember, you're looking for passion beyond mere acceptance and lip service. A smirk can be deceiving, however. If you encounter someone who seems suspicious of your purpose, she may have been burned by a former employer's false or manipulative mission statement. In that case, you need to demonstrate the authenticity of your own purpose. The same applies to you if you're interviewing for a team position. If the interviewer does not raise the subject, do so yourself.

Strong matches also instill loyalty. As my publishing colleague Michael told me, the top editors at Wadsworth often found themselves pursued by competitors who wanted their talent on their own teams. But not even the possibility of a huge salary increase could lure them away. During interviews with rival companies, Wadsworth's editors would always probe for a purpose that paralleled the one Jim Leisy had shaped for the company. If they didn't see it, then no amount of money could persuade them to jump ship. The company's purpose touched them that deeply.

Resonate with Core Identity

A great team purpose shouldn't just tap into your teammates' life stories, it should burrow deeply into the very core of their identity. Back when I was working for a large manufacturing company with a profit-sharing program that rewarded employees through a generous bonus structure, I witnessed a stunning example of purpose at work. People from both of the company's two major divisions had convened to hear both divisional leaders speak. The leaders sketched the usual aspects of a business strategy, including the essential financials. At the end of the presentations, each of them tried to finish on a highly motivational note. The first to speak, a veteran named Roger, tried to pump us up by exhorting us "to work really, really hard so we can take home those big bonus checks." The audience clapped with little enthusiasm. But Geno, the other divisional leader, closed his presentation with: "I want everyone in this company, no matter what your job or pay level, to experience the American dream. I want each and every one of you to feel the satisfaction of owning your own home, of sending your children to good colleges, and of retiring with financial security. Let's work really, really hard to make this a reality." The audience, mainly blue-collar workers, gave Geno a standing ovation. Clearly, his words had resonated with their life scheme, and I could feel all that energy and high emotion bouncing off the walls.

Geno's statement of purpose also struck me to my core because I had grown up hearing the story of how my grandfather had left his impoverished home in Italy, at the tender age of 17, to build a better life in the United States. Many people sitting around me could tell similar stories, including workers who had themselves come from India and other parts of Asia to pursue the American dream. Talk about a match between purpose and life scheme!

Both Roger and Geno cited the same factual information about the company's financial results, but only one of them found the words to inspire us to work, as both men put it, "really, really hard." One spoke to our heads; one burrowed into our beating hearts. We'd follow Roger to the bank, but we'd follow Geno to hell and back. My friend Michael felt the same way about Jim Leisy.

When you define a team purpose with your team, dig deep below the surface. Get to core emotions. You want your purpose to stir people's hearts and reverberate with their identity. Performance and financial goals won't do it. Values and meaningful contributions will.

Build on a Meaningful Theme

Some industries lend themselves to great purposes more than others. It's pretty easy to define a great purpose for a health care, social services, or educational enterprise; it's not so easy to do it for a waste management company. Still, every company on the planet delivers something of value to its customers. Otherwise, it will not stay in business for long. Take a waste management company. Suppose it hauls and disposes of a million tons of garbage a year. Does that fact inspire its people? No, but "We make neighborhoods safer and more sanitary for thousands of businesses and households" might. To define the most inspirational purpose for your team, focus on how the team satisfies real human needs.

The following table can get you thinking in the right direction about the needs that your own team might satisfy. Note the emphasis on values and meaningful contributions to customers and the world, rather than on such mundane acts as reaching sales goals, producing products with zero defects, or hitting quarterly or annual financial goals.

Themes That Satisfy Human Needs

Theme	Human Needs That the Team Satisfies	Most Applicable Industries
Demonstrating Passion for the Product	Design novel products that enhance peoples' lives.	Aeronautics, education, technical services
Providing an Exemplary Customer Experience	Fulfill customer expectations for an ideal experience.	Travel, food service, entertainment, technical services, education
Protecting the Environment	Reduce consumption of massive amounts of natural resources.	Manufacturing, utilities, transportation, forestry, mining, construction
Promoting Public Safety	Alleviate threats to people's well-being.	Utilities, transportation
Empowering the Individual	Deliver information and tools that release people's creativity.	Telecommunications, publishing, technical services
Contributing to Personal Freedom	Provide products or services that people desire.	Fast-food chains, tobacco products, alcoholic beverages
Making Vital Products or Services More Affordable and Accessible	Lower the cost of expensive products or services.	Retail, airlines, construction, communication, health care, professional services, travel, education

(continues on next page)

Uplifting the Lives of Employees	Improve the lives of large numbers of people who earn low wages.	Food services, construction, retail, manufacturing, transportation
Empowering Employees to Create Important Contributions	Provide mental challenges for highly skilled knowledge workers.	Information, technical services, finance, scientific services, entertainment

You can easily think up a great theme for a textbook publisher or a pharmaceutical company because those companies satisfy needs we all admire: education and good health. But even companies with questionable products satisfy real human needs. Companies like Philip Morris and Anheuser-Busch, the large brewing company, make it possible for people to exercise their personal freedom and engage in activities that they enjoy.

A great practice is to have the leaders of the company establish the theme for the overall company and then to have each team define their unique purpose that helps accomplish the company's theme. Teams engaged in different functions within the company might dedicate themselves to their own specific themes or subpurposes. For example, the marketing and sales teams at Philip Morris could embrace the corporate theme of enabling personal freedom but would develop a subpurpose that emphasizes maximizing the customer's experience or providing a variety of products that will satisfy a broad range of customer tastes. Human resources might add a dedication to uplifting the lives of all employees through industry-leading benefits and generous profit sharing.

DEFINING TEAM MEMBERSHIP

David Travers works as the Finance Manager for Universal Community College. UCC's administration has set a rather lofty purpose for the school: "to help community members become good global citizens." To fulfill that purpose, UCC offers a wide curriculum designed to help students understand global cultures and succeed in the realm of global business. David's own team pursues its own subpurpose within this larger framework: "to help UCC achieve its purpose by providing affordable services to all students." His team concentrates on keeping tuition and fees as low as possible without sacrificing the quality of the school's offerings. As UCC grows, David realizes that he needs to expand his team to provide additional services, including a purchasing agent who can negotiate the best cost/value from vendors, an accounts payable processor to manage vendor invoices, and a financial analyst to examine tuition costs and develop creative funding solutions. This brings him to an important consideration. Should he add these roles to his existing team, or should he procure the new services from another UCC internal team or an external service provider? Most financial managers would prefer the former approach because it would protect their turf and keep the new recruits firmly under their control. David, however, has been schooled in the art of developing and leading primal teams and knows the importance of aligning all team members with a strong purpose.

Before he decides on the best option, he asks a pivotal question: "Will these new roles fit solidly within our current team purpose?" With respect to the new purchasing agent, he weighs his choices. Given the fact that vendor supplies and services represent 40 percent of the college's costs, and a good purchasing agent will lower them, that role will make a huge difference to the team's purpose. By pursuing the affordability purpose, the new recruit can use it as leverage when negotiating with vendors, insisting, "We can't afford to pay your customary price because that would force us to jack up tuition for our students." Similarly, the financial analyst's role should also fit snugly with the current team and organizational purposes. The analyst will figure prominently in the team's mission by doing the math needed to figure out how much students can afford to pay for tuition and fees. That person will also look for alternate sources of funding, such as county bonds or federal financial aid. Both of these roles belong on the internal team. But what about the accounts payable processor? Although David wants to hire a skilled player who can do the work accurately and efficiently, a job-well-done will not contribute significantly to the UCC and team purposes. It's important but not integral. Not even the world's very best accounts payable processor will make the sort of difference he expects from the other two positions.

That fact leads David to think about the best solution. Can he find someone working in the school's existing administrative services to do the job? Or should he procure that function from an external vendor? Someone who already works for UCC would already understand and embrace the school's purpose, perhaps with the subpurpose "to provide administrative efficiency for our community college." Drop the phrase "community college" from that purpose, and it could describe the mission of any excellent external provider. In fact, "to provide maximum efficiency for all of our clients" could inspire people at Perfect Accounting Services (PAS) to do a truly outstanding job at the same cost.

In the end, David hired two new people to work side by side with his team, but he farmed out accounts payable to PAS. The moral of the story? When hiring for a team or expanding a team, always take membership into account. Will the role contribute substantially to the team's purpose? Will the candidate for a new or existing job make a good member of the team? Could the results you need come just as well, if not even better, from a member of another internal source or from an outside vendor? Bad membership decisions can undermine your team's efforts to do an extraordinary job. Good ones can propel everyone to great results. Mission accomplished!

Align with Meaning

Ed Tronick, a distinguished professor of psychology in the College of Liberal Arts at the University of Massachusetts Boston, says that when an engaging and meaningful purpose draws people together, they feel exuberant and fully alive. Their minds expand, and their thinking widens. In contrast, when people come together without a meaningful and uniting purpose, they can easily fall prey to negative feelings such as fearfulness and anxiety. Their minds constrict, and their thinking narrows.[9] Exuberant people innovate; anxious people do not.

You don't need a psychologist to tell you this happens. We've all experienced it. When we feel like an outsider and lack any meaningful relationship to the group, we seldom experience the optimal emotions we need to perform at our best. If David had added an accounts payable processor to his team at UCC, he or she probably would not have felt like a fully engaged member when it came time to brainstorm ideas about lowering tuition. Driven by the desire to maximize the efficiency of the accounting system, that sort of expansive thinking could easily make this individual feel like an outsider, not a good feeling for an important player in accomplishing the UCC and team purpose. On the other hand, that individual might feel at home with the birds of a feather over at Perfect Accounting Services, with its all-out focus on accounting efficiency.

In my own case, I've always worked in the field of information technology and know firsthand the difference between tight and nonexistent bonds to a company's purpose. On one occasion, I led an application development team at a logistics company with the express purpose "to provide the best service experience in the industry." Working directly with clients, I could clearly see how my work matched the company's purpose. I felt a strong bond with the company and really loved my job. Later, however, I moved to a new position at the same company where I managed a team devoted to maintaining the organization's technical infrastructure. Our unwritten purpose involved keeping all the machines up and running at the lowest cost. My role no longer differentiated the service we provided to customers, and my bond with the company weakened. The more I felt like an outsider, the more my enthusiasm waned.

Have you drawn a sufficiently clear membership boundary for your team? That boundary should make it clear to everyone that they belong to the group. To paraphrase the old country and Western song, "You need to know when to include 'em, know when to exclude 'em, and know when to let them walk away from the team." The included will do great work, whereas the excluded can walk away to do great work elsewhere, possibly for an external provider of services for your team or organization. That's win-win-win for all concerned.

Organize by Purpose

A team's purpose should profoundly drive the way team members do their work and provide daily inspiration for all team members to do their best. It should fuel a sense of camaraderie. To help ensure strong feelings of belonging, you need to do what David did. As a first step, use the questions in the following table to determine whether the functions performed on your team play an integral role in accomplishing your mission.

Purpose Alignment Questions	
Does the Purpose ...	**Do People Readily Agree That ...**
Provide meaningful direction toward doing the best possible job?	The purpose helps me decide the best way to do my job?
Inspire people to do an extraordinary job?	I feel tremendously energized to get results that fulfill our purpose?
Provide people with a meaningful reason for doing the job well?	When I do my job well, it makes a substantial difference in how well we achieve our purpose?

If you answer yes with respect to a given function, keep it on the team. If you answer no, look at a way to procure the function as a service from a team whose purpose better matches their work. When organizations and teams align by purpose, everyone feels inspired to do their best work. Trying to get great results from misaligned parts is like trying to get milk from a turnip. It won't happen.

USING THE FIVE WHY'S TO DEFINE AN INSPIRING PURPOSE

We have talked about the importance of mining beneath the surface of *what* we do to unearth *why* we do it. "Why does what we do matter to me, my team, my company, and the world?" Continually asking this question can lead you to answers that ignite and sustain team energy. As you hammer out and refine a meaningful purpose, continually ask why what you're doing matters until you identify how your work fulfills a basic human need. That will help you fashion a purpose that inspires your team at their very core.

You can use the following blank template to guide your ongoing exploration of this crucial issue. Ask the why questions over and over until you finally forge your own gold standard for inspiration.

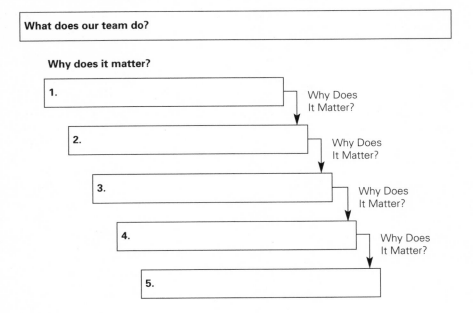

To make sure you and your team think as broadly as possible, periodically revisit the purpose-broadening questions discussed earlier in this chapter.

Here's an example of how this exercise could have looked for Wadsworth Publishing.

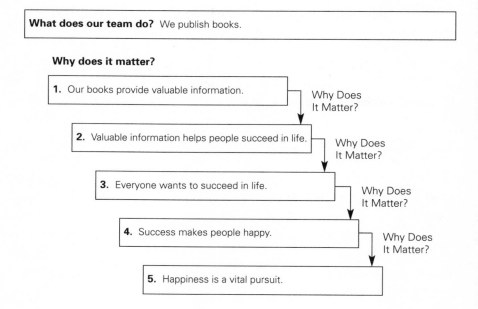

If Wadsworth's leaders had conducted this exercise with their teams, they might have ended up with this purpose: "to empower people in the pursuit of happiness with the books we publish."

CHAPTER 7

Primal IQ

Activating Insight and Intuition

Jerry Knight, the new Vice President of Innovation at Spiraling Technologies, has accepted his boss's challenge to come up with a half dozen new ideas to boost the company's market position. With ample funding for two new positions, Jerry hires two ideal candidates with MBAs from Harvard and Stanford and tells them to "start innovating." The new recruits, Frank Silva and Lena Gold, settle into their plush new offices and set to work, gathering input on customer needs from the marketing department, consulting with the company's engineers, debating the best ways to provide greater value, and drawing fancy diagrams on a huge whiteboard.

Almost a year later, Frank and Lena have wallpapered their office with Post-it notes and turned the whiteboard into a big blot of color that looks more like a Jackson Pollack painting than an innovation plan. To Jerry's chagrin, however, they have not handed him a single idea he can take to his boss, who constantly reminds him that Spiraling's competitors are widening their lead.

In this chapter, we'll explore two surprising facts supported by the latest research in neuroscience: the best breakthrough ideas don't spring from logical thinking, and the most spectacular innovators do not learn their tricks at prestigious business schools. All those intuitive gut feelings that defy logical explanation, those flashes of insight while you're dreaming or smacking a tennis ball around the court, account for more great ideas than all the comfortable couches, Post-it notes, and whiteboards in the world.

LEARNING TO WORK CREATIVELY

Paula Scher, an identity and branding expert highly regarded for her creative abilities, has come up with a lifetime's worth of great ideas, including Citigroup's umbrella logo, the window panes graphic for Microsoft Windows 8, and the Museum of Modern Art's imposing letters. Like many highly respected creative minds, Scher attributes her ideas to the incredible power of insight.

Scher compares her creative process to a slot machine. A lot of stuff whirls around inside her brain: her life experiences, all the books she's read, all the movies she's seen, all the people she knows, thousands of hours of conversations, and every piece of artwork she's ever studied. All that raw material occupies one side of her brain. The other side of her brain holds the specifications for her client's branding project. When she pulls the handle on her mental slot machine, she releases her conscious control over finding the best solution, and her unconscious mind takes over, with everything stored in her brain spinning around like a tornado. Eventually the spinning wheels stop, and a solution pops into her conscious mind. With luck, three cherries line up, and she hits the jackpot with a brilliant idea.[1]

Conventional business thinkers, steeped in the logic and mathematics taught in business school or in on-the-job training programs, scoff at this analogy. It sounds too much like magic. Why spin your wheels when you can most quickly get to your destination by proceeding along a continuous path? After all, you're just tackling a business problem, and like an algebraic equation, you can best solve it by following the prescribed sequential steps to the correct solution. But this old-school way of thinking works only in situations over which we can exert conscious control. Creativity and innovation resist such control. That's why the best ideas often arrive when you let go of the handle and let the whirling machine get the job done.

Get to Aha! by Letting Go

Does that mean that the creative process defies all attempts to harness it? Actually, no. In 1926, Graham Wallas, an English social psychologist and London School of Economics cofounder, came up with what has become the accepted description of the creative process. His theory, based both on Wallas's own empirical observations and on the accounts of famous inventors, proposes that the creative process occurs in a series of predictable stages. It unites both the conscious mind of the conventional thinker and the unconscious mind of the slot machine player.

In a nutshell, it works like this. When we take on a challenging problem, we may spend a lot of time and effort clarifying the issue and trying out different solutions. This activity internalizes the problem into our subconscious mind, where it incubates without further conscious input. As it incubates, all that data may coalesce into a solution, which may dramatically burst into our consciousness as an Aha! or Eureka! flash of inspiration. Then our conscious mind can take over again as we proceed to verify and work out the details needed to implement the idea and share it with other people.[2]

Even if you have never thought a lot about the origin of your best and brightest ideas, those breakthrough solutions to your most nagging problems, you've certainly experienced your own Aha! moments. You're lying in bed early in the morning, not thinking about much at all, or you're jogging down the street, paying scant attention to anything but putting one foot in front of the other, when—*Bam!*—out of nowhere, a great solution that has been eluding your conscious mind for days suddenly pops into your mind. Aha! You may have noticed that an insight more likely occurs when you consciously let go of the problem.

Until recently, many scientists saw no fundamental difference between the Aha! moment and any other cognitive process. But in the April 13, 2004, edition of the *Public Library of Science Biology*, Mark Jung-Beeman (professor of psychology in the Cognitive Neuroscience Program at Northwestern University), Edward Bowden (senior research associate at Northwestern University), and John Kounios (cognitive neuroscientist and Drexel University professor) reported that a specific area of the brain "lights up" when the Aha! moment arrives.

Using brain-imaging techniques, the researchers examined the effects on the brain when participants grappled with 144 word problems, some of which required insight and some of which lent themselves to logical analysis. The imaging equipment revealed increased activity in the right anterior temporal area of the brain when a subject used insight to solve a problem. The right anterior temporal area makes connections among distantly related bits of information during comprehension. The sudden flash of insight associated with the Aha! effect occurs when thinkers make connections that previously escaped them. The scientists also placed nets of electrodes over the participants' heads to measure electrical responses that flicker and flare across the brain's surface. This approach revealed a sudden burst of high-frequency neural activity beginning 0.3 seconds prior to an insight. This gave the researchers a picture of the actual creation of a new idea. Immediately following the neural spike, the new idea pops into the person's consciousness, and they experience an Aha! moment.[3]

During a flash of creative insight, your brain switches into a distinctive mode that occurs only when you consciously let go of the problem and allow your subconscious mind to go to work forming associations between and ultimately identifying patterns in a veritable mountain of far-flung data. In this way, we can process vast amounts of information more efficiently than we could with our conscious minds. Let the conscious mind take a nap while the subconscious mind unveils amazing solutions to big problems.[4] That's exactly what Paula Scher does when she tackles a big branding problem. She pulls the lever on her virtual slot machine and lets her subconscious rove among the mountain of data stored throughout her brain until, "Aha! I see an umbrella for Citibank!"

Letting go of a problem does not mean ignoring or forgetting about it. We must remain passionate about finding the perfect solution. We keep yearning for an answer, periodically revisiting it with our conscious mind to ask, "Have I found it yet?" If Paula hadn't felt deeply passionate about finding a superb logo for Citibank, she might have settled for a logical solution, perhaps an uninspired Monopoly game hotel icon. Albert Einstein put it nicely when he said, *"It's not that I'm so smart, it's just that I stay with problems longer."*

Loosen Up on Efficiency

Conventional business practices do not easily accommodate the way the creative process actually works. In the traditionally mechanistic view of business, leaders view productivity and process efficiency as the Holy Grail. However, in a 2011 issue of *Public Library of Science One*, doctoral student Richard Chi and Professor Allan Snyder, both from the Center for the Mind at the University of Sydney, offered their opinion that the propensity for speed and efficiency actually makes people less receptive to solving problems with creative insight. They see a cognitive trade-off between the need to perform routine tasks well and speedily and the ability to hit upon new ways to do that work.[5] Picture Tony, a customer service representative at Homeward Appliances, a huge consumer appliance store. He focuses so intently on efficiently processing customer returns that he will probably never gain an insight into ways the company might reduce the number of returns. But if he lets go of his all-out commitment to efficiency, he just might get that sudden flash of insight he needs, suddenly shouting, "Aha! I see it! We need to improve the product descriptions in our sales brochures so customers buy the right products in the first place."

Gregory Berns, a distinguished professor of neuroeconomics at Emory University, as well as the author of *Iconoclast: A Neuroscientist Reveals How to Think Differently*, calls the brain "a lazy piece of meat." He bases his surprising characterization on the notion that the human brain has evolved for efficiency and routinely takes perceptual shortcuts to save energy. Perceiving a situation in the usual way requires little energy, he argues, but looking at it from a fresh and novel perspective takes a lot of effort because it forces a thinker to work harder. He says that we should bombard our brain with a lot of unusual combinations of data and ideas, suggesting that only by forcing our brains to recategorize information and move beyond our habitual thinking patterns can we begin to imagine truly novel alternatives.[6]

This argument implies that we can increase team creativity by encouraging members to engage in activities designed to pull them out of their ruts. This can mean doing something as simple as injecting some variety into a daily routine. Let's say that, one Monday morning, as the store manager for a Homeward Appliances outlet, you tell Tony, the fellow in charge of processing customer returns, to shake up his routine. You tell him to interview customers who have brought an unsatisfactory product to the service desk and to fill out the return form himself instead of asking the customers to do it. This activity will make the return process more time-consuming (i.e., less efficient), but the onerous task will cause Tony to think differently, forcing new connections between certain brain cells. If it bumps him out of his rut, he may devise new ways to reduce returns. Now imagine doing that with your whole team, getting everyone in the store to handle a task differently. Performing work in a different way can inspire the sort of thinking that results in novel solutions to problems that everyone has been taking for granted. Although productivity may decrease in the short run, if people come up with bright ideas, profitability will likely rise in the long run.

INCUBATING AN INSIGHT

Sometime around 250 BCE, King Hiero II supposedly ordered Archimedes, the brilliant Greek mathematician and physicist, to determine the gold content of the king's laurel leaf crown. The king suspected that a dishonest goldsmith had mixed some less costly silver with the gold. At first, the problem baffled Archimedes. He could not use the conventional method for measuring the purity of the crown's gold because that would mean melting it down, forming the molten metal into a cube, and measuring its density. Destroying his master's crown could cost him his head.

Stumped by the problem, Archimedes did what any sensible person would do: He took a long hot bath to take his mind off the problem. As he lay back in the tub, he noticed the water rising as his body displaced the liquid. A bolt of insight struck the frustrated mathematician's brain. "If I merely immerse the crown in a vat of water," he thought, "I can easily determine its volume from the amount of displaced water and thus the density and the purity of the gold." According to legend, the elated Archimedes ran through the streets naked, shouting "Eureka!" (That is Greek for "Aha!" or "I have found it!")[7]

When you need to come up with a creative solution to a problem, you probably use a problem-solving strategy that has served you well in the past. But even the most effective customary strategy can eventually turn into a rut. That's when you take a metaphorical "long hot bath" and let the problem simmer in the incubation chamber of your mind. Just when you least expect it, as you lie there drifting away to the sound of Beethoven's Fifth Symphony wafting through your headset, Eureka!, an inner lightning bolt of insight strikes. Incubation is the mother of great ideas. You can't consciously control when that flash of insight will strike you or your teammates, but you can consciously integrate effective incubation periods into your work processes, making it much more likely the inner lightning will strike when you need it the most.

Take a Break

In the *Creativity Research Handbook*, published in 2012, Rebecca Dodds, Thomas Ward, and Steven Smith, all professors of psychology at Texas A&M University, review the experimental research that has been conducted on the relationship between incubation and creative problem solving. After taking a close look at 39 experiments performed by researchers since 1938, Dodds and her colleagues concluded that incubation really does work. Roughly 75 percent of the experiments showed that problem solvers who spent some significant time away from the problem not only hit upon a novel solution but did it more quickly.[8] When your own boss asks you to come up with a truly original thought, you may need to spend some time away from the problem. At IBM, that might involve something as conventional as a coffee break or, at Google, something as unconventional as an hour in the playroom. Even people working in the most buttoned-down environment can do with an occasional visit to a local park or gym where they can put a problem completely out of mind for a while.

Why does taking a break prompt creative solutions? Interestingly, even the experts don't agree, although a few suggestions make sense. A time-out:

✓ Helps your subconscious mind sift through all the possibilities.

✓ Allows your impatience and frustration to subside.

✓ Invites stimuli from new activities and situations into your consciousness.

✓ Makes it easier to shift to a different problem-solving strategy.[9]

✓ Sets the stage for a bolt of inner lightning.

Whenever your team needs to find a creative solution, build a break, a time-out, a change of pace, or a little downtime into the process. Take a few minutes for a game of Texas Hold 'Em in the break room, or go for a brisk walk around the block. Aha! loves to visit your brain when it stops all its fussing and fighting. You just need to do it at the right time.

Get the Timing Right

Good results depend on good timing. The Dodds, Ward, and Smith summary of creativity research indicated that breaks work best after a thinker has gathered comprehensive information pertaining to a problem and has thought fairly deeply about it. You don't launch the team's search with a break. You call for the time-out after the group has explored all possibilities and reached an impasse.[10]

As the team leader, you should consider the need for exquisite timing. Don't do it too soon, before they've done any deep thinking, but don't wait for them to hit the wall and completely give up in utter frustration. Burnout never solved a difficult problem.

Back at Homeward Appliances, suppose you've asked your sales team to spend the next three weeks coming up with a way to reduce the number of products returned by dissatisfied customers. "Collect all the returns data for the past two years, organize it by type of product and manufacturer, look for patterns, and think about ways to cut returns by 30 percent," you ask of them. Taking a break at this point to clear everyone's mind before tackling the task will accomplish little, if anything. Wait until they have come up with at least one good idea, such as eliminating products with high return rates. If at that point the team cannot think of anything else, suggest that they bail out of the office for a little while and do something fun. When they return sharp and refreshed, you may hear some pretty bright ideas. "Boss," says Wally, "I was walking down Broadway yesterday when it hit me! Why don't we do what car dealers do and encourage our customers to test-drive a product before they buy it?" Note the emphasis on fun. If you tell folks to take the rest of the day off to think harder about the problem, they will probably remain at an impasse.

Engage in the Right Activity

A 2013 BBC documentary, *The Creative Brain: How Insight Works*, shows how a certain kind of break can boost a person's creativity. Researchers told volunteers to compile a list of uses for a brick. The subjects thought about it, made their lists, and then, at the urging of the researchers, took a break from the project. During the break, each participant engaged in one of three activities: sitting quietly, sorting a pile of building blocks by color, or building a house with the blocks. The researchers then asked the volunteers to think of even more creative uses for the brick. The people who did the rote task of sorting blocks did best in the second round, thinking of many more possibilities, whereas the people who built little houses, a more demanding task, came up with the fewest. Those who sat quietly fell between the two.[11]

So what do you say when you tell your Homeward Appliances team to take a break? Take a nap? No. Go out for coffee? Nope. Play a round of Trivial Pursuit in the break room or toss around a football in the parking lot? Yep, that might work. They should do something that arouses them enough to take their mind off the problem but not something so arduous it requires their full concentration. Playing a game or tossing around a ball can provide just the sort of Mama Bear activity that can set the stage for inner lightning to strike. But don't take my word for it. Research on working memory proves the point.

Simone Sandkühler, of the Department of Neurophysiology and Center for Brain Research at the Medical University of Vienna, and Joydeep Bhattacharya, of the Department of Psychology at the University of London, have found that since our working memory can hold only a finite amount of data at a given time, we need a kind of gatekeeper to control our use of this limited space. When we concentrate on a certain task or problem, our working memory reaches its full capacity and the gate closes, effectively blocking access to other data from our long-term memory. The gate also restricts input from the external environment. At this point, the mind reaches an impasse. However, when we let our attention wander by engaging in a less intense activity, the gatekeeper allows our mind room to restructure the problem either by searching long-term memory for concepts or existing knowledge about the problem or by receiving external input.[12] In other words, loosening of concentration fosters the Aha! moment.

When the Homeward Appliances team needs a respite from its concentration on the returns problem, they should engage in the sort of fun, playful tasks discussed in Chapter 2, perhaps engaging in a ping-pong tournament or a drumming circle. These types of activities will distract the team from the problem while loosening their attention enough to let their minds restructure the problem and pave the way for the arrival of the Aha! moment. As a side benefit, these activities will also recharge their emotional batteries.

Switch from One Problem to Another

A break can occur without pausing the problem-solving process. You can get the positive effects of a break without actually taking time away from work if you instruct your people to work on multiple problems at once. This allows one idea to incubate while the team concentrates on another one. In the October 2008 issue of the *Creativity Research Journal*, Flora Beeftink and Wendelien van Eerde of Eindhoven University of Technology and Christel Rutte of Tilburg University reported what happens when test subjects switch back and forth between three different and rather challenging word insight problems. The researchers set up three groups, giving each 18 minutes to solve the three problems. The "continuous scenario" group worked for six minutes on one problem before turning their attention to the next one. The "interrupted scenario" group worked on one problem for three minutes before tackling the next one. At the end of nine minutes they started over, trying to solve each problem one at a time for another three minutes each. Finally, the "break scenario" group freely switched among the problems.

It turned out that the break scenario group solved 29 percent and 11 percent more problems than the continuous scenario and interrupted scenario groups, respectively. This supports the idea that break time need not involve time away from problem solving, just respites between different problems. An Aha! moment may arrive for one issue while the team is busy discussing another.[13]

Back at Homeward Appliances, you might add a completely different problem or two to the mix, encouraging the team to switch among the problems at will. Now they can choose when to think about streamlining the returns process or reducing the number of returns or designing more informative sales brochures that inform customers of the pros and cons of a given product. Wally may get his flash of insight about the first problem while mulling over the second, while Sarah might get hers when her mind wanders to the third problem. Wally's idea for solving the first problem may stimulate a related idea in Raoul, who suddenly sees a way to solve the first two problems with one innovation.

TAPPING INTUITION

Bob Lutz, president of Chrysler in the 1990s, tapped his intuition to turn the auto giant around. Looking at the company's stagnating sales, he trusted his hunch that a sexy, outrageous sports car would turn heads on the street and get people excited about Chrysler again. When the company's designers showed Lutz a clay model of such a vehicle, which later became the Dodge Viper, a little voice in the back of his mind convinced him to go full speed ahead with the idea.

Hardly anyone at Chrysler agreed with Lutz. The bean counters argued that the company should invest the projected $80 million in cost elsewhere, perhaps to pay down the company's debt or refurbish its plants. The sales force warned that no U.S. automaker had ever succeeded in selling a $50,000 car, especially to Chrysler's traditional clientele of blue-collar workers who would turn their backs on a car priced over $20,000. Even though Lutz could cite no hard, cold research to justify his hunch, he persevered, pushing the project forward with unwavering commitment.

The Dodge Viper became a smashing success as it single-handedly changed the public's perception of Chrysler, dramatically boosting company morale and providing the momentum that the automaker sorely lacked, ultimately spurring its impressive turnaround in the 1990s. In hindsight, intuition knocked logic for a loop. Later, when Lutz fielded a question about his bright idea, he could only say, "It was this subconscious visceral feeling. And it just felt right."[14]

Call them gut feelings, instinct, or intuition; we all get them. But first-class innovators get them a lot. Amazon's Jeff Bezos and Virgin's Richard Branson chalk up some of their best business decisions to the same sort of subconscious visceral feeling that told Bob Lutz to put the Viper on the road.[15]

For our purposes here, we'll define intuition as the moment a person senses information and makes connections between pieces of information that lie beyond the realm of conscious knowing. It strikes suddenly and seems perfectly valid the instant it happens. It does not follow the pattern of analytical thinking that plods from A to B to C and, finally, to Z. It differs from insight, which, by our definition, involves a period of incubation before reaching a sudden understanding of a good way to solve a problem. However, intuition does follow its own special patterns.

Detect the Patterns

Intuition can reveal ideas that reside in our subconscious but have not yet drawn our conscious attention. Whereas our conscious mind can process only 40 bits of information per second, our subconscious mind, which holds a record of everything we've ever experienced in our lifetime, can process 20 million bits of information per second.[16] Unlike our conscious mind, it never sleeps. It always keeps percolating beneath the surface of our awareness. When it bubbles to the surface as intuition, the body comes into play as much as the brain.

In 1997, Antoine Bechara, professor of psychology at the University of Southern California, published an interesting article in *Science* magazine that demonstrates the relationship between the subconscious mind and the body. For his study, he selected subjects to participate in 100 trials involving a computerized gambling task. In each trial, a subject chose one of four decks of cards displayed on a computer screen. In the midst of the decks appeared one upturned card. Could subjects correctly guess whether the color of the upturned card would match the color of a card drawn from their chosen deck? A correct guess increased a subject's winnings; a wrong guess meant a loss.

Unbeknownst to participants, the computer had predetermined the outcomes from each deck, awarding correct guesses six out of 10 times for decks C and D, but only four out of 10 times for decks A and B. Choosing C and D led to overall profits; selecting A and B led to eventual losses.

Throughout the trials, researchers connected the guessers to skin conductance devices that gauged their sweat gland activity (a measure of emotional response). After sampling all four decks and before suffering any losses, subjects preferred decks A and B and did not show significant changes in skin moisture. After encountering a few losses in decks A or B, usually by the time they reached trial 10, participants began to sweat more when they chose decks A and B and began to avoid those decks. This effect increased through trial 20, when researchers interrupted the game, asking the guessers if they had figured out what was going on. No one could. To the researchers, that meant the subjects had not consciously realized they were going to lose if they picked decks A and B, yet they were subconsciously avoiding those decks. By trial 50, however, most of the guessers expressed a "hunch" that they should avoid decks A and B. By card 80, many said that they "knew" they should avoid A and B and choose C and D instead.

These results imply that subjects subconsciously recognized that certain decks would hurt the chances of winning long before that fact rose into their conscious minds. What propelled them from ignorance to a hunch and finally to knowledge? A bodily signal, increased perspiration, told them to steer away from choices that would reduce their winnings. This nicely illustrates the notion that our intuition influences our decision making before we become aware of it.[17]

Let's see how this applies to Homeward Appliances, where Perry leads a team of appliance buyers. Every spring and fall, his team makes decisions about which new products to purchase, perusing brochures from manufacturers and studying sample products. Throughout the year, they hear thousands of comments from customers about their likes and dislikes, read detailed sales reports showing what has sold and what has been collecting dust on the shelves, and study the multitude of reasons why customers return products. They have stored a million little details in their subconscious minds, but when it comes time to make decisions, they cannot possibly access all of that Big Data with their conscious minds. Luckily for them, their subconscious minds contain it all and can pump out an intuition based on that whole warehouse of stored data. A sense of expanding energy or a burning in the pit of their stomach may signal that they should harken to their intuition. Tony suddenly realizes, "I just know customers will snap up that black refrigerator with the bottom freezer, but we'd better skip that metallic blue washer and dryer set. Those would sit on the showroom floor for months." Given the fact that Tony's intuition usually gets good results, neither Perry nor the team needs a logical explanation. "He's just clairvoyant sometimes."

Predict the Future

Compared to the average businessperson, successful serial entrepreneurs can more easily intuit how a *random* event will pan out in the future. Researchers from the Australian Graduate School of Entrepreneurship, led by Professor Emeritus Murray Gillin, and the Institute of HeartMath, led by Dr. Raymond Bradley, have been investigating the proposition that nonlocal intuition accounts for this phenomenon. By "nonlocal intuition" they mean predicting a future event based on information that does not come from prior experiences or memories, either subconscious or conscious.

The results of this research, published in a 2008 edition of *Regional Frontiers of Entrepreneurial Research*, indicate that successful serial entrepreneurs experience a physiological response that predicts future occurrences. In their study, the researchers placed successful entrepreneurs in front of a computer screen that displayed a series of random photographs. Subjects wore both a skin conductance device and a heart rate monitor. Five to ten seconds *before* the computer displayed a certain photograph, the entrepreneurs' bodies responded to the anticipated photograph. If they predicted an alarming image, such as a snake poised to strike, their skin became moist and their heart rate jumped. They showed few, if any, physiological changes when they foresaw a calming image, such as a puppy romping in a field.

Before you dismiss this research as some sort of crazy voodoo or impossible magic, you might look into the theory the researchers developed to explain their findings. It involves quantum holographic fields, a subject far too complex for our discussion here.[18] Their theory may or may not prove scientifically valid, but try to keep an open mind about it. After all, 50 years ago the idea of a portable personal computer with access to the Library of Congress seemed like a very farfetched idea.

The folks at Homeward Appliances would love to own a crystal ball that enabled them to peer into the future. Now, suspend your disbelief for a moment. Suppose a new supplier, SpaceClean, comes along with a futuristic appliance that combines a washer and dryer in one machine and looks like a flying saucer. Logic would tell the team not to order it. But some faraway inner voice whispers that this contraption may well become the gold standard for home laundry. Five years down the line, that voice may prove prophetic as Homeward becomes the number one seller of machines using the SpaceClean technology. Did the company rely on a crystal ball or spooky magic? Stay tuned as researchers keep exploring the next frontier of neuroscience.

Make the Mind-Body Connection

According to Gerard P. Hodgkinson, professor of strategic management and behavioral science in the Business School of Warwick University, our emotions reflect our intuitions. In other words, an intuition is not a cognitive experience but rather a reaction involving the *entire* psychological and physiological system.

Our bodies create somatic signals that indicate the validity of an idea or a choice. If we're considering a bad choice, our system reacts the way it would to any negative event: Our heart rate goes up, our stomach may begin to burn, and our skin gets clammy. When we weigh a good idea or a sound decision, we experience a sense of expanding energy and comfort throughout our whole body. These signals, activated by emotion, influence our awareness and decision making.[19]

If you want to foster beneficial team intuitions, you must pay attention to team emotions. Obviously, passion engenders innovation. All sorts of thoughts and ideas constantly swirl around in your teammates' conscious and subconscious minds. When they strongly desire optimal solutions, they will find that the most creative and elegant ideas generate the most intense and accurate sensations in their bodies.

Perhaps successful entrepreneurs come up with the best ideas simply because they maintain a strong emotional desire to discover innovative ideas. That passion makes their bodies more attuned to sensing great ideas.

Wanting to strengthen his teams' intuitive decision making about purchases, Perry infuses them with the deep desire to make the right choices. When Traynesha deeply yearns to make the right decisions, when it truly matters to her, she'll much more accurately detect the quality of ideas than will Giovanni, who puts in his eight hours day-dreaming about his passion for golf and feels no differently about appliance X than he does about appliance Z. The same applies to Bae, who fears the consequences of not making the right choices. Fear derails intuition. You can't sense a good idea when negative emotions flood your body.

Traynesha personally resonates with Homeward's purpose. When her team tackles a tough problem, they apply an array of techniques to promote optimal emotions. She can feel her body light up when she thinks up a good idea. Once, as her team was brainstorming how to increase sales, she suddenly felt a jolt of energy traveling up her spine as she hit upon the idea of installing a home theater in the showroom, where customers could relax and watch videos of appliances in action. A year later, the appliance theater has become a popular destination for shoppers.

MIXING IT UP

Conrad Hilton, founder of Hilton Hotels, relied on hunches to make his fortune. His finely tuned, uncanny intuition struck him (and others) as downright spooky, although he denied any real psychic talent. It famously came to his aid when he sought to buy a prestigious old hotel in Chicago. All of the potential buyers were invited to place sealed bids on the table. The hotel would go to the highest bidder.

Some days prior to the deadline, Hilton sealed up a $165,000 bid, but that night he went to bed feeling restless and did not sleep well at all. The next morning he changed his mind. "It just didn't feel right," he said afterward. Increasing his offer to $180,000, he anxiously awaited the outcome. Sure enough, he beat out his closest rival by a mere $200. This deal eventually netted him millions of dollars.[20]

Although you might love the idea of putting highly intuitive people on your team, you need to realize that not everyone possesses this ability. In addition, a team consisting of seemingly psychic individuals would not necessarily achieve spectacular results every time it tackled a problem. You need to mix it up a little.

Know When to Trust 'Em, Know When to Bust 'Em

In a 2008 article in the *British Journal of Psychology*, Gerard Hodgkinson argues that all people possess a certain degree of the primal, innate ability to make good intuitive decisions. He thinks it may be a genetic benefit that evolution has shaped over many millennia. If caveman Ned An-derthal could read danger in a saber-toothed tiger's fresh tracks in the snow, he might avoid becoming its next meal. His descendants would thank him for that intuition! Still, while all people may have been created intuitive, some become more intuitive than others.

People who have experienced more patterns in their life and work will more likely intuit which new ideas will work and which will fail. If Traynesha has worked at Homeward Appliances for 12 years, she's immersed herself in a lot more customer experiences than Giovanni, who came aboard three years ago. Her ability to have hunches has evolved to the point where she sometimes seems as clairvoyant as Conrad Hilton. Does that make Giovanni less valuable? Not a bit. He worked ten years in the home decorating field and brings to the Homeward team intuition about trends in interior design that reflect customer tastes. Bae seems to lack even an inkling of intuitive ability, but he can analyze a problem with impressive skill. Wisely, Perry has mixed some Baes with his Trayneshas and Giovannis.

Hodgkinson reports that people bring varying degrees of intuitive ability to the table and that no one can precisely gauge an individual's intuitive skill. The popular Myers-Briggs Type Indicator (MBTI), designed to measure psychological preferences in how people perceive the world and make decisions, contains a measurement intended to gauge whether a person prefers intuitive information gathering and decision making, but, according to Hodgkinson, it does not result in an accurate measurement of that preference. Hodgkinson would advise Perry to study what Traynesha does on the job. Does she rely on her intuition a lot? Is she usually right? If so, she may be his best intuitive hunch maker.[21]

Interestingly, Barnaby Dunn, a senior investigator scientist at the Medical Research Council Cognition and Brain Sciences Unit in Cambridge, United Kingdom, reported in a 2010 article in *Psychological Science* that research suggests some people's bodies generate the wrong signals. When they considered a bad choice, their body signals miscommunicated it as a good choice. This happened in only a few subjects, but it does drive home the point that you can't trust all of your people's intuitions all of the time.[22]

Again, Perry can only observe and record. As he watches his people apply their intuition and notes the results of a long history of intuitive decisions, he'll develop his own intuitive ability to know when to listen to Traynesha's flash of insight and when to pay attention to Bae's analysis. In short, mixing it up gets better results than relying solely on one dependable oracle.

Balance Decision-Making Styles

Here's a nice team mix: a highly disciplined logical and analytical thinker, a structured thinker given to occasional flashes of insight, a keenly insightful person who can apply logic when needed, and a died-in-the-wool intuitive. For a primal team leader, it's a balancing act. Sometimes a problem demands the skills of the logician; sometimes it needs to incubate in the mind of a structured thinker before an Aha! moment strikes; sometimes it requires a perfect blend of intuition and logical analysis; and sometimes it takes the team "clairvoyant" to dream up the best solution.

Intuitive processing runs like a rabbit and can leave analytical processing eating its dust. Then again, that slow tortoise can also win a race. The swift rabbit gets good results on unstructured problems, where a hunch comes quickly without a lot of logical dilly-dallying. The slow tortoise, planting one foot in front of the other, gets good results on structured problems, where a methodical step-by-step approach gets you more efficiently to the finish line.

If Perry's team needs to determine how many refrigerators the company needs to buy for fall sales, they should use Bae's analytical approach based on the hard facts of historical sales and future forecasts. But if they need to determine which new models will add pizzazz to the lineup, they might listen more closely to Traynesha's intuition. Then again, an accurate final sales projection for the full line of products may take an equal measure of both.

Also, people can switch between intuitive and analytical modes of thinking. Hodgkinson would say that a Traynesha could come up with spot-on hunches one minute and perfectly sound numerical analysis the next. People are people, not pegs that fit one hole and one hole only.[23]

USING THE HUNCH DETECTOR TO SENSE INTUITION

This tool will help you engage your intuition and your team's when making decisions. Keep in mind that when consulting the body's intuitive input about whether a certain decision will prove right or wrong, it must fall into one category or the other. There is no half-good/half-bad option.[24]

Step 1: Prepare to Intuit.

- Reduce any negative emotions with the techniques in this book.
- Reach a state of coherence by following the instructions in Chapter 1.
- Set aside hard data and other distractions and just listen to your body.

Step 2: Perceive Your Body's Signals.

While holding a solution or decision in your thoughts, notice how your body feels:

How a No Signal Feels	How a Yes Signal Feels
• Decreasing energy	• Expanding energy
• Tightening of the muscles	• Tingling muscles
• Burning in the pit of the stomach	• Feelings of health and vitality
• Heaviness in the limbs	• Warmth spreading across the chest
• Depression of overall mood	• Brightening of overall mood
• Pain in the stomach, neck, chest, or head	• Sensation of comfort throughout the whole body

---

Remember the unpredictability and changeability of all human beings. Getting good at applying intuition takes patience, perseverance, and trial and error.

Step 3: Build a Repertoire of Knowledge over Time.

- How do you feel when an option turns out exceptionally well?
  - What signals do you experience throughout your body?
  - Does the signal move from one area of the body to another?
- How do you feel when an option turns into a disaster?
  - Where in your body do you experience the signals?
  - Does the signal move from one area of the body to another?

CHAPTER 8

Team Spirit
Building Emotional Bonds

Recently promoted to director at a large software company, I was look-ing forward to attending my first leadership retreat. I'd wondered why the retreat coordinators had asked me to submit two pictures of my fam-ily a few weeks earlier, but when I walked into the conference room that morning I found my answer. Pictures of my husband and me with our dogs on the beach flashed across a huge video screen to the accompani-ment of the uplifting song "In the Living Years." I stood there with my heart in my throat as my family photos shuffled among those of the other leaders.

Everyone stared at the screen. No one uttered a word. It's hard to express all the feelings that flooded my mind and body at that moment. Pride, certainly. Happiness, of course. And, to use a word you seldom see in a business book, *love*. The family-like bond that formed that day between me and the other leaders in the company fortified us through many years of tough challenges and hard work and accounted for much of the tremendous success we built during the subsequent years.

We've all seen or heard about teams in sports, music, the military, or business that turn in performances transcending the ordinary. Somehow, each team member overcomes any personal performance limitations and attains an unprecedented level of energy and ability. What drives such team spirit, and can we intentionally create it?

In this chapter, we'll examine the emotional bond that forms in the most elite teams and explore proven ways to generate it in any team.

TIGHTENING THE CONNECTIONS

When new hires at Beryl Companies, a call center business in Bedford, Texas, show up for their first day of work, they know right away that they're working in a special place. When they arrive for work, they stroll through a human "tunnel" built especially for them by current employees. The veteran workers form two long lines, lift their hands high in the air, and cheer and applaud each new recruit as they make their way through the tunnel. This simple gesture jump-starts the bond between the new hires and their teammates, and it heightens the mutual bond felt among *all* employees.[1]

Most coworkers relate to each other at the surface level, where they see each other as both comrades who share the workload and, at times, as competitors vying for rewards and advancement. Some may bond more deeply and become good friends over time, but for a team to unleash its maximum creativity and full potential, everyone must relate at a deeper, personal level.

Generate Mutual Care

When teammates relate to each other with a genuine feeling of care, they satisfy a primal need. According to Roy Baumeister, the eppes eminent professor of psychology and head of the social psychology graduate program at Florida State University, and Mark Leary, professor of psychology and neuroscience and director of the Social Psychology Program at Duke University, we all yearn, at a fundamental level, to feel a sense of belonging with other people. This sense of community arises when we experience a personal bond, cemented by care and trust and emotional concern, with our teammates. We want more than a mere work relationship, where we feel only a loose affiliation with our coworkers. We crave deeper, more personal relationships, the kind that fuel optimal emotions, ranging from delight and joy to contentment and calm. When we interact regularly with people with whom we don't feel a strong sense of belonging, we often end up with potent and even toxic negative feelings, including fear, anxiety, depression, and loneliness.

I cared deeply about the well-being of all my teammates at the software company I mentioned earlier and knew that they felt the same way about me. However, I have also worked on teams where dissimilar feelings and unequal levels of concern thwarted or weakened relationships and prevented bonding. A team grows strongest when each person feels a reciprocated emotional bond with each and every teammate.[2]

When your team members see each other as people worthy of compassion and concern, not just as coworkers sharing a workplace, they begin to bond. A team leader can do a lot to help the team take their relationships beyond the surface level of their work and connect at a more satisfying, primal level. It's not easy because many people feel reluctant to expose their personal selves, especially in the early stages of their work with new colleagues.

I've often used what I call a Pecha Kucha event to create the atmosphere of mutual care and respect that stimulates even the most reticent member of a team to open up to the others. Pecha Kucha refers to the Japanese event where pictures appear in rapid succession on a screen. I invite each team member to provide five or six photographs of themselves, images that capture who they are and that "move their soul" or "give their life meaning," along with short descriptive captions for each photograph. When I present the slide show to a team, I flash each of the photos for six seconds. Imagine the scene. People get really excited as they see flashes of a colleague smiling on his wedding day, romping in the surf with her dog, standing between his parents on graduation day, crossing the finish line at the Boston Marathon, or just making a funny face at the camera. Even people who have worked with each other for many years discover something new about a teammate. "I never knew you work holidays at a homeless shelter!" "Wow, that is one ugly cat!" "Aw, you were such a pretty baby!" The event gets people interacting and laughing, but more importantly it leaves everyone feeling more deeply connected to their teammates, often without realizing it.

Sharon runs Hearthstones, a popular restaurant that serves simple comfort food. She oversees a team of six kitchen staff, eight wait staff, and one bartender. About a month ago, she facilitated a Pecha Kucha event at one of her all-hands-on-deck monthly meetings, after which she posted the various pictures on a big bulletin board in the staff break room. It doesn't take long for Sharon to see a heightened sense of camaraderie among her people. They share more personal stories, they offer to pitch in with a helping hand when a coworker spills the soup, and they generally express a lot more compassion and concern for each other. Everyone learns that gruff head chef Arnulfo is a caring father of five, not just the uncompromising taskmaster who rules the kitchen with an iron hand. Arnulfo discovers that Cari, the new waitress, dreams of becoming a psychotherapist specializing in family issues as she juggles her part-time waitressing job with her studies. He now understands why she sometimes seems distracted at the beginning of her shift. He treats her a little more gingerly during that first hour and has even asked for her advice about a problem with his teenage daughter. And Cari now sees a big, warm heart beating beneath Arnulfo's gruff exterior. Everyone, Sharon included, feels happier coming to work and tackles all the daily problems, which erupt in any busy restaurant, with a lot more gusto and creativity.

These good feelings at Hearthstones arose because Sharon made a deliberate effort to create a heightened sense of connection and belonging among all her people. She captured their hearts and, as we'll soon see, their brains.

Extend the Trust

Paul Zak, a neuroeconomist at Claremont Graduate University in Claremont, California, says that when our interactions with other people engage our emotions and make us feel compassionate or empathetic, the chemical oxytocin surges in our brain. Oxytocin (not to be confused with the prescription painkiller oxycontin) is a small molecule, or peptide, that serves as both a neurotransmitter, sending signals within the brain, and as a hormone, carrying messages in the bloodstream. When oxytocin surges, people become more cooperative, more generous, and more caring. That's what Sharon observed in her people at Hearthstones. Our brains also release oxytocin when someone shows trust in us.

Paul Zak drew these conclusions from numerous trials of what he calls a Trust Game experiment. The experiment exercise involves two scenarios involving monetary exchanges between an investor and an anonymous trustee. In the first scenario, the investor starts with $10 and can choose to transfer some or all of it to an anonymous trustee. This initial exchange triples the transferred sum, so if the investor transfers the whole $10 to the trustee, that sum immediately becomes $30. The trustee then decides how much, if any, to pay back to the investor. Despite the fact that the anonymous trustee can keep all the money without fear of repercussions, Zak found that most investors left the game with substantially more money than their initial $10. Why did the trustees behave so generously, when they could have pocketed all of the profits? The next scenario sheds some light on that behavior.

In Zak's second scenario, the investors did not decide for themselves how much money to transfer to the trustee. Instead, they picked a random number out of a bucket. In both scenarios, the trustee knew whether the investor or a random pick had determined the amount. When trustees received transfers of money based on the investor's own decision to trust them, their oxytocin levels ran 50 percent higher than when they received money based on random chance. Furthermore, the trustees returned twice as much money when they knew their benefactors had chosen freely. The researchers found a close correlation among level of trust, the amount of oxytocin released, and the percentage of gains returned to the investor. This study clearly supports the contention that generosity depends on a bond of trust between two parties.[3]

A bond of trust lays the groundwork for other positive human emotions, including caring, cooperation, respect, admiration, and even love. It also engenders creativity. Because creativity depends on taking risks, we tend to do it much more ardently when we totally trust our teammates for support and backup. Only in such a truly trusting environment do we feel safe offering our most daring, innovative, and outrageous ideas.

But how do you instill trust in a group? You begin by placing your faith in them. Over the years, I have made this my motto: "Expect people to do the right thing, without the need for a lot of rules." These words visibly light up a team. They resonate. And they get results.

In a lot of big organizations, rules abound. Many of them, such as human resource regulations, arise as a reaction to a mistake. A lawsuit over sexual harassment leads to a whole host of rules about gender in the workplace. At Hearthstones, a table of six customers walked out because it took too long for Cari to take their order. Sharon could have laid down the law with a new rule: "Every server must take every customer's order within five minutes of their being seated." But instead, Sharon talked with Cari about what happened and gained her commitment to improve her timeliness. This took care of the issue without burdening the whole team with new rules.

Whenever I have shown teams that I trust them, I have seen fairly immediate results. People no longer show up late for work or meetings, and they don't need prodding to put in extra hours to complete a project on time.

In stark contrast, a fat book of rules and regulations tells people, "Since we don't trust you to do the right thing, we've put together this manual that tells everybody what to do, all the time, in every conceivable situation." That message will make everyone feel distrusted, disrespected, resentful, and indignant. It motivates people to stop thinking creatively, to cover their tails, to avoid admitting mistakes, and, in the long run, to settle for lackluster results. It all happens deep inside our brains.

According to Paul Zak, trust triggers oxytocin and oxytocin prompts prosocial behavior. In other words, when someone trusts us to do the right thing, our brains naturally release oxytocin, which prompts us to act for the good of the team. Back at Hearthstones, Sharon trusts her team to do the right thing and, as a result, finds her people cooperating more freely and displaying a lot more team spirit. She even puts Zak's findings to work. She informs her team that she is eliminating an old rule, set by the previous manager, that the wait staff must put half of all their tips into a tip pool divided among the rest of the staff, including those who work in the kitchen. "I trust you to contribute a fair portion for those who help you do your jobs so well," she says. Two weeks later, Chef Arnulfo tells Sharon that the amount he can split among the kitchen staff has actually increased. From her reading about neuroscience in the workplace, she knew that this happened due to a rise in the wait staff's oxytocin levels. Cooperation in general has gotten a boost. Joe no longer argues with Holly, the hostess, about seating the most lucrative parties in other sections because he trusts her to distribute high tippers equally around the room. Joe pitches in to help newcomer Cari more often by refilling coffee cups or delivering checks to her tables. Even the customers notice the cheerfulness of the whole staff and respond accordingly, with higher tips.

Oxytocin gave a big boost to the folks at Hearthstones, but it can also backfire in certain situations.

Lengthen the Ties That Bind

Jennifer Bartz, adjunct assistant professor of psychiatry at Mount Sinai Hospital, cautions that oxytocin doesn't always create optimal cooperation and generosity. Her review of oxytocin literature, published in a 2011 issue of *Trends in Cognitive Science*, revealed the variable nature of its effects on cooperative behavior. It turns out that the care and trust it promotes do not apply to the world at large, but only to a person's close associates. Some studies have even shown that oxytocin actually decreases collaboration outside the immediate team. If you're leading a team inside a larger organization, your team members may become tight-knit but less inclined to work collaboratively with others in the organization. Cliques don't mix.

Bartz and her research team propose that oxytocin causes people to pay more attention to social cues and become more keenly aware of whether or not someone outside the team is a friend or foe. Increasing people's attention to social cues will naturally strengthen social bonds with familiar allies but diminish them with anyone perceived as a potential enemy.[4]

Sharon has created a tight-knit team at the main Hearthstones restaurant, but when she asks Joe, her best server, to lend a hand at a newly opened branch location across town when a flu epidemic strikes, he balks. "We're competing for some of the same customers!" says Joe. "If they're short-staffed, we just might pick up some customers. We offer the same menu." Sharon realizes he views the people at the new location as competitors. "But they're our sister operation," she pleads, hoping to convince him to view the one across town as an extension of their own group. To make that happen, she takes Joe aside and spends some time helping him feel an affinity toward Phillip, the manager of the new restaurant. She tells him about Phillip's passion for creating an inviting atmosphere for customers as well as employees and how she has used some of his ideas in the main Hearthstones location. She also shares that she and Phillip have agreed to share staff across their locations so that all employees can take a vacation this year. As a result, Joe starts to feel a budding kinship with Phillip. After all, he's a member of the Hearthstones' extended team. Now Joe agrees to lend a hand to the sister operation.

Extol External Threats

According to Baumeister and Leary, the researchers who investigated the nature of community bonds, external threats also increase team cohesion and the tendency to form strong bonds. A landmark study of World War II veterans' groups provides convincing evidence of the power of an external threat to pull people together. Four decades after the war, soldiers who had experienced heavy combat together and suffered the deaths of close friends still felt extremely strong bonds with their former comrades. In contrast, soldiers who had experienced combat but not the deaths of those close to them felt much weaker bonds 40 years later. Both groups, however, retained stronger ties than those in units that had not seen actual frontline combat.[5]

Herb Kelleher, former CEO of Southwest Airlines, mastered the art of using external threats to bond his employees to the company and to each other. During orientation, every employee watched a movie depicting the history of Southwest Airlines. In it, the recruits saw that Southwest had started amidst fierce competition and conflict, fighting not only competing airlines but the State of Texas for its very life. In Kelleher's memos, speeches, and personal interactions, he persistently underscored the fierce competition in the airline industry and shared stories about Southwest's bitter battles over the years. When the company was fighting to keep its operations at Dallas's Love Field, he inspired his troops to write letters to the city council, circulate petitions, and attend city council meetings. All of this effort built a tremendous *esprit de corps* throughout the company.[6]

Sharon takes a cue from Kelleher and keeps her team apprised of any new restaurants that encroach on their territory. "Mario's! Look at their buy-two-get-one-free on pasta dinners," Sharon says, brandishing the Mario's flyer. "Our pasta dishes make theirs look like dog food. Let's make sure we don't lose customers to those upstarts." This them-versus-us mentality draws her people into an even tighter circle. But could this sort of bonding ever get out of hand?

AVOIDING COMMON BONDING PITFALLS

"How could we have been so stupid?" President John F. Kennedy asked after realizing the infamous Bay of Pigs invasion in 1961 had failed so miserably. His administration had approved the ill-fated plan by a small band of Cuban exiles to cross the Gulf and overthrow the Castro government. Within days, the enemy had killed or captured the entire invasion force and forced the U.S. government to send food and supplies to Cuba in order to ransom the survivors. In the end, the invasion turned into a major foreign policy disaster for the administration.

In 1972, Irving L. Janis, a research psychologist at Yale University and a professor emeritus at the University of California, Berkeley, analyzed the Bay of Pigs disaster and concluded that Kennedy and his team had suffered the consequences of groupthink, a distorted style of thinking that occurs in cohesive groups and renders them incapable of making a rational decision. Janis argued that Kennedy and his team should have seen the huge flaws in their plan, but they were so blinded to reality by their team unanimity that they heedlessly proceeded with it. The team members listened only to one another and had, as a result, thoroughly reinforced a false sense of invincibility. No way could such a brilliant plan designed by such an ingenious team possibly fail.[7]

Bonding may lift up a team, but too much bonding can also bring it down. How do you reach a happy medium between too little and too much?

Candidly Discuss Major Decisions

In 1994, Brian Mullen, professor of psychology at Syracuse University, led a review of all existing research on the relationship between group cohesiveness and effective decision making. Specifically, the researchers set out to determine the validity of Irving Janis's claims about groupthink. The results of their review appeared in a 1994 issue of the academic journal *Small Group Research*.

The researchers had found convincing evidence that poor decisions can result from a team placing an overriding emphasis on consensus and mutual support. However, this problem crops up primarily when the team functions in a "clubby" atmosphere in which members gain more prestige from working on an elite team than from creating a great work product. They found that teams can mitigate the negative effects of groupthink by carefully considering various alternatives to achieving a goal or solving a problem.[8]

At Hearthstones, Sharon comes up with the idea of creating a children's play area in a corner of the restaurant, believing it will attract more families. Several staff members privately worry that it could ruin the restaurant's cozy but upscale ambience. But because no one wants Sharon to think they don't support her or aren't good team players, they don't voice their concerns. Fortunately, Joe suggests they institute a decision-making process that will ensure that the group raises and discusses any major decisions about the business. With this approach, they will feel they can safely express and consider dissenting views. When Sharon hears her team's reservations about the play area idea, she abandons the idea, saying, "Thanks for your honesty, guys. What was I thinking?"

Challenge Each Other

After Sharon adopts Joe's process for vetting ideas, she can then focus her attention on generating more grist for the mill. How can she make sure her people keep thinking of ways to improve the business? Given the dynamic and volatile nature of the restaurant business, with new establishments and creative cuisines constantly popping into the local market, Sharon needs great new ideas to remain competitive and keep growing the business. Like most leaders, she considers scheduling periodic brainstorming sessions for her staff. Before she does that, however, she might heed the advice of experts who have discovered ways to get the most out of such sessions.

Keith Sawyer, an associate professor of psychology at Washington University in St. Louis and author of *Group Genius: The Creative Power of Collaboration*, believes in the power of brainstorming but proposes that it works best when coupled with solitary creative thought. Sawyer says that decades of research have consistently shown that brainstorming groups think of far fewer ideas than the same number of people who first work alone and then later pool their ideas.[9] Have you ever participated in a brainstorming session where people constantly throw out ideas? You can barely think through the ideas that you want to express because other people are interrupting your thought process with their own ideas. You can reduce such disruptions by asking people to spend some time alone thinking about the challenge before the meeting. In that way, team members can weed out less worthy ideas and bring only the soundest ones to the session.

Most people believe that during brainstorming, you should obey the motto, "There is no such thing as a bad (or dumb) idea." Well, some ideas really *are* dumb. But after some debate, a seemingly silly or ridiculous idea may lead to a brilliant insight. In 2003, Charlan Nemeth, professor of psychology at the University of California at Berkeley, divided 265 female undergraduates into teams of five. She posed the same problem to all of the teams: "How can traffic congestion be reduced in the San Francisco Bay Area?" She then imposed one of three conditions on each team. The first set of teams received the usual marching orders about brainstorming, including the no-bad-idea rule. The second group of teams was instructed to say whatever popped into their minds but also to debate and even criticize each other's ideas. The third group received no instructions at all and could collaborate in whatever way they chose. All of the teams would brainstorm for 20 minutes.

Can you imagine what happened? The groups that received standard brainstorming instructions slightly outperformed groups given no instructions, but teams that were encouraged to debate ideas came up with 20 percent more creative solutions than the other two groups. Nemeth says the findings indicate that debate and criticism stimulate rather than inhibit ideas. Dissent stimulates new ideas because it encourages us to engage more fully with others and to reassess our own viewpoints. Nemeth adds that even the most wrongheaded alternative views help expand our creative potential.[10]

Sharon, knowing that a cohesive, bonded team can not only withstand but can actually benefit from criticism and debate, tells her people, "Let it all hang out. If we can't fight with each other, how can we fight the competition?" She's right. Never underestimate the power of a good debate. A friendly argument can strengthen bonds and result in that one bright idea that solves the thorniest problem and propels the team most swiftly to its goal.

Keep All Eyes on the Goal

As you work to increase the bonding in your team, make sure that maintaining the bond doesn't overrule other important objectives. This happened in an infamous incident documented by Wayne Boss, professor of management and entrepreneurship at Leeds School of Business at the University of Colorado, and published in a 1981 issue of *Group and Organization Studies*.

Deleting names to protect the guilty, Professor Boss described what happened at a state agency in a major metropolitan area that employed about 100 people. Interpersonal issues between one of the agency's directors and the ten supervisors reporting to him were undermining the agency's performance. To improve the situation, the head of the agency hired a consultant, who conducted a three-day intervention designed to confront and resolve the issues. During the intervention, the director and supervisors identified and openly discussed everything that had been interfering with their work. Both before and after the intervention, the team completed a survey of team cohesiveness. The survey completed after the intervention indicated that bonds within the group had strengthened considerably, which was good news. But then came the bad news: The group's bond with each other had grown far stronger than their bond with their employees.

When the director and supervisors returned to the office, the supervisors would refer employee complaints about another supervisor directly back to their colleague. This betrayal of trust infuriated the complainants but pleased the supervisors, who took pride in their unwavering loyalty to one another, even when the complaint seemed perfectly justified. As a result, relationships between subordinates and supervisors quickly eroded to the point where the subordinates refused to sit down and discuss any workplace issues with their supervisors. Three weeks after the intervention, 16 of the subordinates filed an official grievance with the state personnel office. Within two months, six of the 16 employees had resigned and three more had been terminated. Those who remained became incapable of working productively in what they saw as a hostile environment. The department's work practically ground to a standstill. Eventually, it required a total overhaul. The moral of the story: Do not let a team's bond work to the detriment of the rest of the organization.[11]

Could it happen at Hearthstones? You bet it could. We saw how the team spirit at one location caused workers there to withhold support of their sister operation across town. It could get even worse. If Sharon's team concentrates so hard on bonding with each other, singing "Kumbaya" and telling jokes in the kitchen while customers go hungry in the dining room, the business will suffer. To prevent this from happening, Sharon must keep in mind the danger of bonding for bonding's sake rather than for the sake of team and organizational performance.

This brings up the heart-wrenching subject of firing a chronically underperforming teammate who has bonded with the team. As much as that can feel like a death in the family, such team members eventually impair the team's performance, no matter how much people like them. This is the most emotionally difficult thing I've ever had to do as a team leader, but I knew that if I let poor performance persist, it would eventually sink the whole team. If and when you must cut someone loose, you should do it with the utmost compassion and respect, not just for the sake of that person's feelings, but for the emotions of everyone else on the team.

When Sharon finally reaches the end of her patience with Cari, who simply cannot pick up her pace and keeps gossiping about other staff members despite a half dozen patient interventions, Sharon spends a full hour discussing the transition with Cari. She presents it as an opportunity for growth in another field. Later, she takes each member of the staff aside to make sure they understand that Cari's leaving is in her own best interest as much as that of the restaurant. She puts Cari's situation in positive terms when she says, "She's intent on finding a job better suited to her many talents."

BROADENING PERSPECTIVES

Sometimes you need to obtain a wider perspective on an issue. BASF, the giant global chemical company, developed an innovative, life-saving product by joining together diverse teams. Working together, these teams devised a mosquito net infused with a specially formulated insecticide that not only repelled but killed the pesky, disease-carrying insects. It took the cooperation of employees from different divisions with vastly different backgrounds and perspectives to create this innovative product, now used throughout the world. In Kenya alone, it has already reduced infant mortality in high-risk areas by 44 percent.

The story of how this innovation came about illustrates how people with different mind-sets can combine forces to come up with ideas that each person alone might never discover. It took a bold move to make it happen. The people who worked for the two key teams from the textile and insecticide departments had seldom engaged with each other in the past. Historically, those in the insecticide division thought only about creating the next great chemical to keep bugs at bay, while the textile division workers focused all their energy on developing new materials with a practical function. However, when BASF started promoting diversity and inclusivity practices to get employees from disparate groups to work together and share ideas more frequently and fruitfully, the two groups proved that sometimes one plus one can equal three.[12]

Recent research on how the human brain functions has shed light on why people with different perspectives can assist each other to come up with the most innovative ideas. These insights have led to a set of practices that can help diverse teams achieve amazing breakthroughs.

Experience a Different Reality

In *The General Theory of Love*, authors Thomas Lewis (assistant clinical professor of psychiatry at the University of California, San Francisco, School of Medicine), Fari Amini (professor of psychiatry at the University of California, San Francisco, School of Medicine), and Richard Lannon (associate clinical professor of psychiatry at the University of California, San Francisco, School of Medicine) point out that each of us possesses a neural perspective that defines how we see the world. That point of view arises naturally from the information that the human brain stores in patterns of brain cells called neurons. Every thought consists of neurons connecting, or firing, in a certain sequence. Those that fire most frequently become closely bound together to form the distinctive neural pathways that give rise to our particular perspectives.

As a case in point, let's consider the perspective on food that has grown in the mind of Arnulfo, the head chef at Hearthstones. Born in Mexico City, he grew up in a poor family and always associated food with comfort and survival. Thus, during his early experience his neurons fired in such a way that, even now, thoughts about food naturally trigger emotions that activate thoughts of substantial, filling meals made with basic, economical ingredients. To him, that's the very definition of food. Period. The thought of a flamboyant, fusion cuisine meal made with exotic ingredients would never occur to him. As a result, he's created a menu of home-style comfort foods, including roasted meats, mashed potatoes, and gravy and biscuits. He doesn't even like to add a parsley or shaved carrot garnish to the plates because he thinks of it as a waste of food. His mother would *hate* that.

Arnulfo's thoughts about food have become deeply ingrained in his brain. The neural patterns established over time keep firing the same way. When Sharon tells him she thinks he should consider adding some flair to the menu by introducing a few new and appealing items, he immediately thinks of adding a new pot roast. He can't imagine anything outside his established patterns. He can't even see the possibility of something like American/Indian fusion cuisine. In his mind, the words "flair" and "food" simply don't fire together. The same thing happens to all of us. A lifetime of ingrained patterns can blind us to really radical alternatives. But rubbing shoulders with people we come to like and who hold different perspectives can, over time, "change" our minds.

When Sharon hires Rajan, a new assistant chef, Arnulfo initially hates the new fellow's suggestion that they put curry sauce on the baked salmon and serve chutney with the biscuits. Over the ensuing months, as Arnulfo bonds with his new colleague, his perspective begins to change. "I never thought I'd live to see the day I'd serve a coriander sauce with the steak," he says.

Break Out of the Ruts

According to Lewis and his colleagues, our perspectives continue to evolve throughout our lives, but the most substantial changes arise from exposure to other people's emotions and ideas, especially those of people with whom we have bonded. That's what it took for Arnulfo to broaden his perspective. No bestselling new cookbook or steady prodding by Sharon could have accomplished as much as his growing fondness for Rajan. Emotions establish our neural patterns, and it takes an emotional connection to revise them. Arnulfo admits as much when he says, "You know, it really opened my eyes when Rajan invited me over for dinner. I ate a lot of weird stuff. But you know something? I loved it!"

Those closest to us most measurably affect our brain chemistry and nervous systems, as our neural connections synchronize with one another. As Arnulfo and Rajan bond, they influence and repattern each other's brains. When Rajan talks about the Indian food he loved as a young boy in Bombay, Arnulfo can sense his experiences and almost taste the food himself. Under his new friend's influence, his neural connections begin to change. As he and Rajan spend more time together, he grows more and more comfortable with the idea of adding foreign tastes to his menu. His whole way of perceiving food shifts. This transition happens so subtly that he doesn't even realize that a truly radical change has been taking place in his head. He doesn't just adopt Rajan's taste in food; he comes to associate food with feelings of flamboyance and spice. This opens him up to different styles of cooking.

At the same time, Rajan's perspective on food has been changing under Chef Arnulfo's influence. "Roast beef and mashed potatoes. I can see why they call it 'comfort food.'" As the resonance between the two men's minds strengthen, they begin not only to appreciate but *feel* each other's different worldviews. Together, they come up with a new style of cooking, an infusion of Indian ingredients and techniques into basic, home-style American cooking. Rave reviews attract new customers. And loyal customers love the new twists that do not abandon what they expect from the Hearthstones menu.

It didn't happen by accident. Sharon made it happen by deploying her skill at bonding her people together into a tight-knit unit. She consciously built the deep connection of mutual emotional empathy that laid the groundwork for her chefs to adopt a shared perspective on cooking.[13] She made sure her people communicated with each other, spoke their minds, argued when necessary, and, most of all, carefully listened to one another's point of view. In this safe environment, people naturally broadened their perspectives without losing their individual differences.

Mix Familiar with Diverse

If you want to promote creativity in a team, you need to assemble and engage diverse people who offer fresh neural patterns to one another. This involves as much art as science. You must take care to get the right mix of people on the team—a combination of like-minded people who are familiar with one another and new people with differing points of view. Brian Uzzi, professor of leadership and organizational change at the Kellogg School of Management, Northwestern University, and Jarrett Spiro, assistant professor of organizational behavior at INSEAD (a highly regarded international graduate business school), set out to determine the optimal mix of familiarity and novelty on teams that produced and performed in Broadway musicals. Their results appeared in a 2005 issue of the *American Journal of Sociology*.

The researchers thoroughly examined a data set that included 2,092 people who worked on 474 musicals from 1945 to 1989. After spending years analyzing the teams behind these productions and their relationships with one another, they found that the thousands of artists they studied enjoyed a vast social network with lots of interconnections. To quantify the density of these connections, the researchers devised a figure they called Q (on a scale of 1 to 5). On musicals developed by teams of artists who had worked together several times before (a common practice on Broadway), Uzzi and Spiro would assign a high Q. A musical created by a team of strangers would receive a low Q.

The researchers then matched a musical's Q ratings with its relative success, based on reviews and financial results. The results contained at least one surprise. As you might guess, a certain Q level did predict success on Broadway. A low one, less than 1.7 on Uzzi's five-point scale, usually spelled failure. It seemed that artists with strong rapport worked well together, whereas those who lacked rapport did not. But then came the surprise. When the Q registered higher than 3.2, the work also suffered. It turned out that the artists involved in those productions thought so much alike that they did not easily come up with innovative ideas that would add pizzazz to the production. The top hit shows came from an intermediate level of social connectivity (between 2.4 and 2.6). A show produced by a team with a Q rating within this range tripled the chances of commercial success over ones produced by teams with a score below 1.4 or above 3.2. It was also three times more likely to win praise from the critics. The lesson for team leaders? Mix it up, but not too much. Diversity plus familiarity breeds success.[14]

The findings suggest that Sharon should create a medium level of connectedness within her 15-member team that might ideally include a total newbie, three or four newish members who have worked at Hearthstones for a year or less, several veterans with more than a year of service, and perhaps one seasoned old hand who has worked there since the beginning. This optimal mix balances the stability of common ground with the richness of diverse perspectives.

USING THE TEAM BONDER TO PROVOKE DEEP CONNECTIONS

You can most effectively get your team connected at a deeper level by setting the stage for strong healthy team bonding. Use the two-step tool in The Team Bonder whenever you form a new team, add new members to an existing team, or just want to deepen emotional connections among team members.

The Team Bonder

---

1. **Get Personal:** For helping people open up, understand, and feel compassion for each other

Technique	Useful Hints
Pecha Kucha—Ask each team member to submit five or six captioned photographs depicting something meaningful about their life.	Present the event in a setting where you can use a computer and projector and where everyone can comfortably gather to watch the show.
Coat of Arms—Invite each team member to prepare a coat of arms that depicts his or her values. The team can present their creations to the group and then add them to a general display.	Note both shared and divergent values. Never make moral judgments, especially about values that stem from racial, gender, or cultural differences.

Best Bosses—Urge the team to describe the best bosses they ever worked for and why they admired them so much.

Personal Profile Introduction— Propose that people introduce themselves as a person, emphasizing *who they are* not *what they do*. Ask them to share something personal about their family, how they spend their free time, and their hobbies and other enthusiasms, such as sports teams and favorite dishes.

Don't take it personally if people cite traits you do not display yourself. Do take heed of traits you wish to acquire or enhance. Make this a fun, interactive event, not a chore. This works especially well in a short session, when you cannot afford the luxury of an extended retreat.

---

2. **Establish Team Norms**: For setting the team's basic operating policies and procedures

Rules and Policies—Keep these to a minimum but clearly communicate the essential ones.

Explain the need for the rules and gather the team's input to clarify them.

Idea Generation—Institute regular brainstorming sessions designed with this chapter's tips in mind.

Make sure people know that you value any and all ideas, from the ridiculous to the sublime. Foster an atmosphere of vigorous yet respectful debate.

Decision-Making Framework— Establish who will participate in which types of decisions, always striving for inclusiveness.

Make sure people know they can and should freely express their views during decision making, even challenging your decisions.

Over time, most groups will develop a surface level of cooperation and harmony, where people comfortably cooperate and treat each other with civility. Left on their own, some teams develop more optimal deep emotional bonds. But why chance it and why delay it? Take steps to create the team spirit we all crave.

CHAPTER 9

The Balanced Culture
Restraining Runaway Egos

Carl Fowler, a sales manager at Engineering Solutions, has built his career by relentlessly trying to outshine his teammates. He's a very bright guy, but in meetings he constantly restates and even takes credit for his teammates' good ideas. As sportswriter Dan Jenkins once said about an egomaniacal film director, "He never lost a conversation." When Jose says, "We need to focus more on implementation and less on strategy," Carl jumps in with, "For weeks I've been saying we've got to stop looking at the forest and start chopping down trees." Jose cringes. The rest of the team roll their eyes and shake their heads. Needless to say, nobody feels very fond of Carl. As Jose sarcastically observes, "He's like a guy walking around with a weather balloon. He can't see around his own ego!" Despite his self-aggrandizing behavior and the fact that the teams he joins never perform as well as expected, ES executives have taken a shine to Carl and keep promoting him.

Leaders cause immeasurable damage when they let runaway egos like Carl's go unchecked. Nothing can diminish a team's bond and energy level as quickly as ego-based separation, where a gulf grows between an egotistical coworker and everyone else on the team.

In this chapter, we will explore just a few dimensions of team culture. By "culture," I mean simply the way we do things around here. Although the topic deserves a book of its own, for our purposes here we will spotlight a few common cultural practices that undermine results because they allow or even encourage team members to act in their own self-interest at the expense of their teammates' welfare. We will also look at alternative practices that help strengthen emotional bonds, maximize optimal team emotions, and create a more vibrant, results-oriented culture. It all comes down to a balancing act.

MODERATING EGOTISTICAL BEHAVIOR

On December 28, 1978, the crew of United Airlines Flight 173 had experienced only routine conditions as they brought their four-engine DC-8 into the Portland, Oregon, traffic pattern. However, as they lowered their gear for landing on final approach, they heard a dull thump from the vicinity of the main gear area. The captain elected to abort the landing. Air traffic control then put the aircraft into a holding pattern until the crew could pinpoint the problem and decide whether or not it warranted further emergency precautions.

For approximately one hour, the captain maintained the plane's holding pattern while the crew tried to determine the cause of the noise. During this time, both the first officer and the flight engineer warned the captain on four separate occasions that the plane was running out of fuel and that he needed to make a decision about landing. The captain brusquely dismissed these warnings and continued to circle the airport. Finally, as the first of the four engines flamed out, the captain aimed the plane toward the landing field. One by one, the other engines failed as the fuel tanks ran dry, and the plane dove toward the ground. At 6:15 PST, Flight 173 crashed into a wooded, populated area killing eight passengers and two crew members, and seriously injuring 21 passengers and 2 other crew members. The National Transportation Safety Board attributed the deadly crash to the captain's failure to monitor the aircraft's fuel state and to respond to the crew members' advisories regarding the dwindling fuel supply. The noisy landing gear, it turned out, would not have prevented a safe landing.[1]

The captain's ego, more than anything else, caused that plane to crash. An unrestrained ego almost always leads to trouble. And it invariably frustrates and infuriates those, like the diligent crew members, who find their input falling on deaf ears. When such behavior becomes the norm for a team, it creates an egocentric culture that will eventually crash and burn.

Create a Culture with a Collective Spirit

Leaders usually seed their business teams with people who possess the best skills and proficiencies, but they often pay too little attention to how well they will work together. If Carl's unchecked ego prompts him to take credit for others' ideas, the team suffers. If he constantly tries to prove his work outshines that of his teammates and consistently discredits their contributions, the team suffers. In the highest-performing teams, every member values and heeds the input of others. A collaborative and respectful approach cements positive bonds, promotes learning, and minimizes mistakes. It could have saved Flight 173. It could have made Carl a hero rather than a disliked adversary on his team. Like so many of the topics discussed in this book, Mama Bear egos work best. Big Papa Bears run roughshod over people; little Baby Bears keep their heads down and their mouths shut.

In a 1992 article by James Driskell, owner of Florida Maxima Corporation, and Eduardo Salas, professor of psychology at the University of Central Florida, published in *Human Factors: The Journal of the Human Factors and Ergonomics Society*, the authors presented research showing that egocentric people do, in fact, hinder a team's effectiveness. They

found that highly egocentric people tend to engage less in collective behavior than people with more restrained egos and that consequently the
latter usually get better results.

The researchers carried out a two-phase experiment to test the effect
of ego on team performance. In Phase One, they identified which of 60
research subjects displayed collective behavior by listening to and acting
on input from others. The researchers also determined which of the 60
displayed the strongest egos and generally ignored the input of others.
Subjects worked in two-person teams and never actually met one another, communicating only by computer. Each team looked at a series
of slides depicting two checkerboard patterns and tried to determine
the largest of each pair. Each team member independently picked either
the top or the bottom pattern. Then the partners compared notes and
made a final choice. The researchers instructed each participant to adopt
their partner's choice as their own if they thought this would help them
make the correct decision. In this phase, both patterns were identical in
size. The resulting decisions showed that each subject fell into one of
three groups: (1) the highly egocentric, who usually rejected their partner's opinion; (2) the more collectively oriented, who usually weighed
their partner's selection; and (3) the least egocentric or altercentric, who
almost always accepted their partner's decision. The researchers excluded
the third group from further study.

In Phase Two, the researchers set up teams entirely composed of either collectively or egocentrically oriented members. They then asked
the teams to perform a decision-making task similar to the one in Phase
One. In this case, the two patterns varied in size.

The results showed that collectively oriented team members improved their overall team performance almost fivefold over their egocentric counterparts. When these team members disagreed, they
changed their answers 40 percent of the time, resulting in better team
performance. But when egocentric members disagreed, they changed
their answers only 16 percent of the time and showed little, if any, enhanced team performance.[2]

Let's imagine how this might play out in a moderately sized police department. Chief of Police Manuel Fernandez oversees a team of six detectives in West Beach, Florida, a recently incorporated and rapidly growing suburb of Miami. About a year ago, he assembled his hotshot detective team by selecting candidates with the best test scores on standardized exams and the strongest go-get-'em attitude. Why, then, do the stats on closed cases over the past year seem so lackluster? The team's closed case record has fallen lower than any other district of Florida, but, even worse, they have not been able to take over half of their solved cases to court due to insufficient evidence.

When Manuel looks more closely at his team's behavior, he concludes that, despite their consummate skills, they simply do not know how to make the most of their partnerships. For example, he notices that two of his detectives, Jolene and Alberto, who are investigating a string of auto thefts, follow up leads and interview suspects as if they are engaged in a competition to outshine each other. Their clashing egos keep slowing down, rather than speeding up, the investigation. They need to learn how to work more as a team and less as a couple of prima donnas competing for the lead role in *Swan Lake*. Luckily for Manuel, he can take some sure steps to imbue Jolene and Alberto with more collective spirit that will strengthen the entire team culture.

Redefine Leadership

The Carl we met at the beginning of this chapter actually worked for me when I served as the chief information officer of a major company in the Northwest. Once I learned of his reputation as a glory hound, I tried to find a way to get him to set aside his desire to outshine his teammates and become a better team player. When I discussed my concern with him, he said something I'll never forget. "If I know my performance will be judged based on whether I'm a good team player, I'll become one. I've never bothered in the past because playing nice never got me big raises or a single promotion." In other words, "If you reward me for individual performance only, why should I become a better team player?" Good question.

It's a bit of a paradox. You promote people with great individual track records, but you expect them to turn in superior team performance. If Jolene and Alberto score big time on their exams and show a lot of take-charge initiative, you promote them to detective. They deserve it, but this strokes their egos even more. Their individual accomplishments, not their team orientation, have won them higher compensation, greater prestige, and more influence. But what if you need a strong, cooperative team in order to solve more cases and win more convictions? Manuel should promote people based on who has done the most to enhance the performance of the entire team. Who has added important improvements to the team's processes and techniques? Who regularly seeks and carefully considers the advice of others? When Manuel includes these questions in his deliberations, he immediately sees that Warren stands out from his fellow detectives. Sure, he's done a good job solving cases on his own, but he's also bent over backward to help the entire team solve more cases. Just last month, he introduced a new forensic technique for determining the source of cloth fibers found at crime scenes. That technique helped other detectives solve four difficult cases. As a result of all this, Manuel promotes Warren to Lead Detective, explaining to the other detectives, and most pointedly to Jolene and Alberto, "Warren keeps showing us that a well-knit rope is a hundred times stronger than a pile of pretty threads."

Warren quickly proves himself in his new position. Given his well-controlled ego and collective orientation, he does not let this promotion go to his head. He demonstrates every day the value of sharing ideas, listening closely to what others say, and enabling the team to do their best work. This inspires Manuel to rethink his basic definition of leadership. He even goes so far as turning the organizational chart for his department upside down, with his position shown at the very bottom. This makes it clear that leadership belongs not to the one who dominates the group but to the people who support it. This in no way diminishes the role of leadership in his organization. It's a tough job to listen to all team members and guide them to get the work done effectively. He knows when to give people a long rope and when to put them on a short leash. He often lets his teams make their own decisions and set their own pace, but when a situation requires a firm hand, he doesn't hesitate to address it resolutely. This style of leadership takes more effort than just barking orders, but that's why he pulls down the big bucks.

Warren's promotion sends a clear message to all of the detectives that advancement and rewards will depend on how well they enhance the success of the entire team. Jolene and Alberto take this "team thing" to heart and talk at lunch about how they can become more effective partners. Remember my colleague Carl? He eventually got the team thing too and became a much more valuable player.

Clip Arrogance at Its Roots

An oversized ego can make for a bumpy ride, but arrogance can completely derail the train. Arrogant people not only discount information from others, they exaggerate their superiority by disparaging others, trying to make their colleagues and subordinates feel inferior by belittling, berating, and browbeating them. When anything goes wrong, it's everyone else's fault for being such complete idiots.

One of the key people Manuel inherited when he took the job as West Beach's Chief of Police was a tough veteran nicknamed Captain Bly, who supervises the work of 14 lower-grade officers. Those who work for Bly have grown to loathe and avoid him because he never misses an opportunity to tell them that they are stupid and incompetent. "We would need only half as many officers to patrol West Beach if you guys were competent," he tells them. "When I was a police officer in Miami, I could spot an armed robber a mile away, but you guys couldn't find Jesse James if he ran over you with his horse." Why, you may be wondering, would a leader act so arrogantly?

In the July 2012 issue of *The Industrial-Organizational Psychologist*, Stanley Silverman, an industrial and organizational psychologist and professor of psychology at the University of Akron, along with several colleagues, published an article about the behavior of arrogant people. Summarizing four years of research designed to answer questions about the nature and consequences of arrogant behavior in the workplace, the researchers found that arrogant individuals don't actually think of themselves as superior to others. Rather, they use arrogance to mask their feelings of inadequacy. Supremely arrogant people, who suffer from low self-esteem and even low intelligence, typically perform poorly on the job. They often fall into a downward spiral. Their fears of inadequacy drive arrogant behavior, and when that behavior elicits negative responses from others, they suffer yet another blow to their self-esteem.

Arrogant behavior poisons the emotional climate of a team because it interferes with productive interpersonal interactions, makes the whole team feel uncomfortable, and inhibits creative problem solving. Worse, arrogant people worry so much about how they compare to others, they forget that they need to improve their own abilities.[3]

What can Manuel do about Bly's behavior? First, he cannot let himself get fooled by the fact that Bly acts far less condescendingly around him than he does around his peers and subordinates. To fully grasp Bly's impact on the team, Manuel has to carefully and respectfully seek candid feedback from everyone on the team, perhaps as part of regular departmental performance reviews. When people know that the opinions of their colleagues will affect their chances to win raises and promotions, they may modify their behavior. At the very least, it will give Manuel the information he needs to deal with Bly's adverse influence on the team.

Manuel can also help Bly fill the gaps in his competency and performance that have made him feel so insecure. He might provide training aimed at improving Bly's deficient leadership and communication skills. In most cases, an arrogant person does do something well. Manuel needs to emphasize Bly's strengths, not just his shortcomings: "You do a great job planning your patrol officers' routes, and you're going to develop into an excellent leader if you can interact with your people in a way that doesn't make them feel belittled or disrespected." Getting Bly to change his ways, even a little bit, will benefit the departmental culture.

BALANCING COMPETITION AND COOPERATION

The Venice String Quartet consists of four world-class musicians. But at least one critic found their recording of Beethoven's *Complete String Quartets* "so out of sync so much of the time that their energy, enthusiasm, and heart don't count for much." Respected music critic James Leonard attributed the flawed performance to excessive competition among the four musicians. According to Leonard, the cellist tended "to go his own way when not taking the lead." When the first violinist took the lead, the cellist did not follow the way he should because he was so intent on showcasing his own talent. "Even with the best will in the world, sooner or later the listener will run out of patience," Leonard concluded.[4]

Whenever talented team players compete more than they cooperate, the team can quickly fall into disharmony. The results that can accrue from positive collective behavior disappear, the team bond wanes as each ego vies to prove it's the best player on the team, and the whole culture suffers.

Stress Mastery Rather Than Performance

Most leaders find it hard to strike the perfect balance between healthy competition and productive cooperation. Although Manuel would never dream of pitting two detectives against each other just to see who finds the bad guy first, he unwittingly creates unnecessary competition when he allows only one lead detective and divides the pot of money for pay raises based on the relative performance of each team member. If everyone wants to become a lead, with all the perks it entails, and desires the biggest pay raise, every member of the team will strive to outshine peers, sometimes at the expense of overall team results. A culture that emphasizes the separate efforts of individuals can't compare to one that stresses the collective effort of the group.

Wait a minute. What about the power of "friendly" competition? Doesn't that sharpen everyone's wits and get them performing at the top of their game? Maybe not. Research by Kou Murayama, lecturer at the School of Psychology and Clinical Language Sciences at the University of Reading, and Andrew Elliot, professor of psychology at the University of Rochester, published in a 2011 issue of the *Personality and Social Psychology Bulletin*, indicates that when workers strive to outdo one another to attain personal performance goals, their *performance* actually suffers. Working memory performs less well, and creative problem solving falls by the wayside. People tend to get better results when they strive to do their best and achieve *mastery* goals. The type of achievement goal you're pursuing greatly affects your perception, attention, and memory. "I'm going to improve my ability to solve armed robbery cases" always beats "I'm going to solve this case faster than Jolene."

Performance goals encourage a narrow focus, where a worker concentrates on doing precisely what's needed to show competence. A detective single-mindedly trying to prove that he's better than others will tend to concentrate almost exclusively on what he needs to solve a case quickly. When Alberto concentrates on finding the auto thief faster than Jolene, he uses all the routine investigative methods, interviewing witnesses, searching for the stolen property, and interrogating suspects. His limited perspective blinds him to other, possibly creative approaches, such as Jolene's suggestion that they explore new cyber research techniques for monitoring the activity of suspects.

Jolene exemplifies the benefits of setting mastery goals, which promote curiosity and exploration and learning. When she sets her sights on becoming a master detective, she'll look at problems through a wider lens, weighing any idea that might sharpen her skill set and help her solve a case. She'll also invite and consider the input of others. This way, she may see clues and possibilities that she might otherwise miss. When she uses a new software program that tracks unusual sales of auto parts, she discovers the name of a man on parole from prison for burglary who has purchased sophisticated tools used to bypass ignition systems. That leads to a quick arrest.

When researchers Murayama and Elliot tested the effects of mastery versus performance goals on long-term memory, they found that the former tend to prompt higher memory recall. From a neuroscientist's point of view, mastery goals seem to facilitate broad-based encoding of memories, whereby the brain stores rich and variable contextual associations it can easily access in the future. Performance goals, with their narrower focus, stimulate fewer of the contextual associations for later access.[5] Given Jolene's dedication to becoming a master detective, she will probably remember more details of the auto theft case than Alberto, who just wanted to solve it quickly so that he could improve his performance statistics. A year later, he has forgotten all about it.

Reward Team Performance

Teammates typically compete for salary increases and bonuses that depend on established performance reviews. If the West Beach budget allows Manuel $40,000 for raises, he would give Jolene a 14 percent raise based on her strong 4.8 rating on a 5-point scale and a 3 percent raise to Alberto with his weak 1.5 percent rating. The better Jolene does, the less money is left in the pot for Alberto. This means that Alberto not only wants to do well but also wants Jolene and his other teammates to do poorly, which promotes a culture of competition in the entire team. There's a better way to reward people, one that balances self-interest with team welfare.

Suppose Manuel wants to use the $40,000 in a way that will increase the collaboration on his team of detectives. So he decides to base raises on team performance, giving everyone a raise based on how well their team met its goals. If his team of detectives meets 50 percent of their goals, Jolene and Alberto and the rest all score a 2.5 out of five points, and if the police officers meet 80 percent of their goals, they all rate a

4.0. In this scenario, each police officer will receive a bigger raise than each of the detectives.

The minute the team of detectives learns that Manuel has adopted this scheme, they step up their efforts to boost the team rating. This means much more collaboration and much less grandstanding. While Alberto used to lay awake at night trying to figure out ways to beat Jolene's arrest numbers, he calls her at 9:00 P.M. to discuss ways they can work together to improve the team's numbers. Former rivals become allies as people start sharing information across cases, inviting and listening to their teammates' input, and relinquishing power to others when it will lead to a better overall outcome. They still work diligently to do their personal best, but not at cross-purposes with their teammates. Before long, Manuel can see a more balanced culture of cooperation replacing the overly competitive one.

How does Manuel make sure he does not damage individual initiative with the new approach to raises? The next year he makes a small adjustment, basing raises 75 percent on hitting team numbers and 25 percent on reaching certain individual goals. For Bly, this means that 25 percent of his evaluation will depend on demonstrably reducing his arrogant behavior.

Don't Arbitrarily Limit the Number of Leaders

In many organizations, a person can progress along a continuum that reflects increasing skills and abilities over time. For example, the job structure for a detective may progress as follows: Probationary Detective in Training, Detective, Senior Detective, and Lead Detective, or levels I, II, III, and IV. People move up these ranks based on merit. Higher ranks indicate higher levels of expertise and achievement. Moving up usually doesn't necessarily mean you start managing people, as, say, a sergeant or captain or lieutenant would, but it does mean higher pay and prestige, as well as potentially higher-level responsibilities. A level III or IV detective may take on additional duties, such as coordinating media coverage or recruiting.

Many organizations limit the number of people who can occupy senior positions at any given time in a particular area, a policy that can lead
to fierce competition for a few coveted spots. If the West Beach Police
Department sets a limit of only one lead detective on the force, the six
detectives may vie quite strenuously for that position. Using a conventional hierarchy, the team of detectives would view the lead as the best
in class, the gold standard for individual performance. However, Manuel
has chosen a team-oriented approach, defining best in class as those who
contribute most to the effectiveness of the entire team. By using that
measure of performance, he can remove the constraint on appointing
only one lead detective. Theoretically, all six could become leaders in
specific areas of expertise. Jolene may become the resident expert on
cyber research, sharing new techniques with the entire team, while Alberto does the same with state-of-the-art forensic techniques, and Joel
becomes the master interviewer of primary persons of interest. Each leads
in one area and follows in others. This brings to mind Emmett Murphy's
definition of leadership in his book *Leadership IQ*: "Every worker leads,
every leader works."

Manuel wisely sets challenging benchmarks for the level of performance needed to earn a lead position. Each candidate must demonstrate a
solid history of introducing new techniques and establishing best practices that measurably help the entire team get results. This system of
rewards inspires terrific performance by the team of detectives because
it stresses collaboration rather than competition. Of course, the detectives will still compete from time to time, perhaps even for Manuel's
job. There can be only one chief of police in West Beach, and many employees may yearn to have that job one day. But Manuel has removed
unnecessary competition from the department.

Establish Broad Spans of Responsibility

Most people love to hone their skills and show off their expertise. To
exploit that aspect of human nature, consider establishing broad spans

of responsibility and accountability. Narrow spans can induce fierce rivalry as everyone on the team competes to rule a small domain.

Manuel encounters this problem when he sees the two officers who patrol the east side of town continuously bickering with the two who patrol the south. South complains that East spends more time in the doughnut shop than behind the wheel of the cruiser; East belittles South for never getting out of their cruiser and walking the streets. South claims superiority over East, and vice versa. Even when Manuel assigns different patrol officers to three slots, the rivalry continues unabated. Oddly, this never happens with North and West. Eventually, it dawns on Manuel that one major difference sets South and East apart from North and West: the former include West Beach's mostly affluent homes and upscale businesses, whereas the latter encompasses the town's poorest and most crime-ridden neighborhoods. Could it be that South and East have too little work to do and waste their overabundance of spare time on unnecessary competition with one another? He tests that theory by redrawing the areas of responsibility for the patrol officers into three sectors that include a better balance of rich and poor parts of town and arranging for the transfer of two officers to the Miami police force. Now the three sets of officers find their work more challenging and end up spending the lion's share of their time doing the job.

Beware, though, that too broad a scope can cause as much trouble as too narrow a scope. When an avalanche of cases slams Jolene, she resents any teammates who seem to have avoided getting buried alive by their work. Make sure you give everyone that Mama Bear level of responsibility that can best satisfy their need for mastery and accomplishment but that does not weigh them down with an unbearable load.

TAPPING THE BEGINNER'S MIND

The late Tibor Kalman, a well-known American graphic designer, had always shunned the notion of becoming an expert at anything. He felt that once people become experts, they quickly lose their creative spark. This reasoning led him not to do the same thing twice. If someone approached him to design a brochure for a museum exhibition, but he'd done one of those already, he'd politely decline and say, "No, I want to design the exhibition," even though he'd never designed an exhibition before. After he designed the animated *Nothing But Flowers* video for the popular music group Talking Heads, he received a lot of calls from television directors. "Hey, Tibor, could you do that typography thing on my commercial?" He would refuse. Didn't people get it? He hated repeating himself just because someone admired his work and would pay him well for it. If he succumbed to that flattery and the chance at an easy payday, he'd end up taking the shortcuts artists take when they routinely practice the same skill day in and day out. Hello rut, goodbye creativity.[6]

Most people don't think that way. They work their tails off gaining in-depth knowledge through constant repetition, honing their skills until they become recognized experts. Author Malcolm Gladwell emphasized the value of this approach in his book *The Outliers*, where he claims it takes someone 10,000 repetitions to master a skill. In a team setting, this sort of expert often wields power over the rest of the group, setting an example for junior teammates to follow. Ironically, these same experts often lose their ability to think up and weigh the wildly creative solutions that can lead to team breakthroughs. Smart beginners resent them for that. Those feelings can lead to team-damaging competition, with the newbies learning fewer conventional skills than they should and the wise old dogs never getting out of their same old rut.

So-called beginner's mind refers to the propensity to approach each situation with openness and few preconceptions, no matter how many times you've encountered it before. When veteran employees approach their work with this mind-set, they can think and act as creatively as the newbies. When they do, they earn everyone's respect. Fortunately, you can take some sure steps to help your people tackle situations with a beginner's mind.

Limit the Power of the Expert

People with the most in-depth knowledge and experience typically prefer the methods that have made them successful in the past and dismiss newfangled approaches they have not tried before. As noted by John Maynard Keynes, the British economist whose ideas fundamentally shaped the theory and practice of modern economics, "The difficulty lies, not in the new ideas, but in escaping from the old ones, which ramify ... into every corner of our mind."[7]

Richard Chi and Allan Snyder, both from the Center for the Mind, University of Sydney, published an article in 2011 in *Public Library of Science One*, an open-access, peer-reviewed scientific journal, that agrees with Keynes. They suggest people get stuck in mental ruts because the human mind is hypothesis driven. We tend to see the world in a preconceived fashion (according to our accepted hypothesis about reality), accepting at face value the information that coincides with our expectations or mental templates and discounting any evidence to the contrary, at least on a conscious level. Even though our hypothesis-driven mind can help us efficiently deal with familiar situations, it can also prevent us from finding the novel solutions that can occur when we look at a situation in an unfamiliar way.

Chi and Snyder conducted experiments to see whether they could temporarily induce in test subjects a state of mind less prone to the influence of mental templates or preconceptions. To do this, they activated or inhibited certain areas of the subjects' brains with transcranial direct current stimulation (tDCS), a safe, noninvasive technique for stimulating brain activity. They decreased excitability of the left anterior temporal lobe (the part of the brain associated with maintaining existing hypotheses) and increased the excitability of the right anterior temporal lobe (the part of the brain associated with insight and novel meaning). The researchers asked subjects connected to the stimulation device and a control group who received no brain stimulation to solve a series of insight problems. When the test concluded, Chi and Snyder found that subjects who had received the brain stimulation successfully solved the problems three times more often than the control group.[8]

Now, you can't go around implanting electrodes in people's heads, but you can facilitate a beginner's mind in everyone on the team by decreasing the influence of experts. When you endow certain people with the power of the expert, you effectively inhibit team creativity. Doing so sets the expectation for everyone involved that the experts know all the answers. Naturally, the experts will fulfill that expectation by providing answers based on their past experience. The other team members, who may have thought up more creative answers, become less inclined to offer their ideas, leading to dampened team emotions and leaving little room for creativity and innovation. When you help people let go of the idea that so-called experts know it all, you open up the team to fresh ideas, help them forge stronger bonds, and generate better results.

When Vivian Stevens, a detective in training, and Alberto, now a senior detective, tackle a missing person's case, her beginner's mind proves invaluable. The case: The parents of a 14-year-old girl named Dana report that their daughter disappeared soon after the family returned from church that morning, over ten hours ago. Alberto's gut, based on years of experience, tells him that Dana has run away from home, possibly with a boyfriend. He's seen it a hundred times before. A girl that age gets sick of her parents' restrictions and decides to break free with a bad boy. Vivian listens patiently to that theory and files it away for future reference. She has looked over Dana's bedroom: a Bible on the nightstand, a portrait of the family's golden retriever hanging over the bed, nothing out of place, no clothes on the floor, no Goth posters, no heavy metal in the CD rack. "Where's the dog?" she asks Alberto. He stares at her for a second. "What the heck has that got to do with anything?" But he holds his tongue while Vivian lays out her own theory. "If we find the dog, I bet we find Dana." Scouting the area, they soon see the family dog nosing around the backyard of the abandoned house next door. When they approach the animal, they can see that it's circling a fairly deep sinkhole. The girl has fallen into the hole and can't get out by herself. Case closed. A year later, Vivian solves another case of a missing girl when she begins her investigation with Alberto's advice in mind: Look for the boyfriend, and you'll find the runaway.

This scenario illustrates the win-win-win effect of balancing experience with creative insight. The team wins, and the customer (in this case, a frantic parent) wins. Manuel set the stage for this triple victory when he limited hierarchical behavior in his organization. All of his team members know that the title of "senior" or even the title of "chief of police" doesn't necessarily confer brilliance and infallibility on someone. Nor do the labels "newbie" or "probationary" automatically make their bearers earth-shatteringly creative. Each can add an important voice to the chorus it takes to get great results.

Get the Old to See Anew

Some people approach each situation with a beginner's mind, an attitude of openness and lack of preconceptions, even when they're highly accomplished professionals. A study led by Shelley Carson, lecturer at the Harvard University Department of Psychology, reported in a 2003 issue of *Journal of Personality and Social Psychology*, found that some of the most creative people display a condition called low latent inhibition (LLI), which causes them to treat each situation with freshness and novelty, no matter how many times they've seen it before. Examining a sample of high-IQ individuals, Carson found creative achievers seven times more likely to act with reduced latent inhibition.[9] This points out the value of getting people to see the same old experience from a fresh perspective, much as a person with LLI does. Get into the habit of exposing your whole team to different perspectives, urging them to look at an old familiar situation or problem as if they had never encountered it before. This puts team members with varying degrees of experience on a more equal playing field, where everyone, not just the newbies, will more likely come up with novel ideas.

For example, try putting your team in the shoes of their end user. If your team runs a help desk, have them call in as a customer with problems. Playing the role of the customer gets the team looking at their processes from the other end of the telescope. They may suddenly see better ways to ask the customer to describe the problem or to improve methods for diagnosing the issue.

Manuel periodically requires that his officers act like ordinary citizens out walking the dog before dawn, strolling through the park late at night, or riding the bus at midnight through not-so-safe neighborhoods. The whole town, which the officers know like the backs of their hands, seems different somehow. When they replace their satellite's-eye perspective with the worm's point of view, they invariably come up with new ideas to increase public safety.

You can also stir up novel insights by shifting responsibilities. If you run a product design team, a day spent answering phones in customer care can open your team's eyes to the needs of your customers. In West Beach, Manuel periodically rotates the patrol officers to different parts of town and occasionally puts detectives in the backseat of a patrol car for a few hours, just so that they can see the town from a patrolman's perspective as well as that of a suspect under arrest. A burglary specialist tags along on an arson investigation, and vice versa. Manuel also likes to team an officer with fresh eyes with one who has seen it all before. Fresh doesn't necessarily mean new to the force but rather new to that part of town or that job or that specialty.

These culture-building techniques help ensure that every team member, not just the newbies, approaches the team's work with a fresh perspective that leads to more creative thinking and better results.

Shake Up Mental Patterns

You can expose your team members' minds to new ways of thinking by challenging their deeply rooted assumptions and forcing them to contemplate fresh points of view. This gets the veterans thinking as creatively as the newbies, while not losing the benefit of their experience.

"The way we do things around here" can grow stale if it devolves into unquestioned conventional wisdom. It never hurts to identify and challenge even your most sacred core beliefs and to shock your team by questioning their faith in them. "What if customers will pay more for better service?" can stimulate ideas for new revenue streams and service improvements. "What if our primary job is to increase public safety rather than to fight crime?" Manuel asks. "What would we do differently?" That whisks the team members out of their customary crime-fighting thinking and into the novel posture of asking themselves what really poses the highest risk to public safety and even how to prevent people from becoming criminals in the first place.

Stir your team members' imaginations by forcing them to compare their group to other seemingly unrelated organizations. "How would Ben & Jerry's improve our media player?" may seem off-the-wall, but it would get people thinking about flavors that would appeal to customers with vastly different tastes. Manuel asks, "How would Google improve our cyber research techniques?" and "How would Apple redesign our community relations program?" This forces people to think differently and come up with ideas that otherwise would not have occurred to them. You can also boost creativity by imposing nonexistent constraints and by asking your team to imagine a world where they must function with those limitations. "What would we do if telephones no longer supported voice communication?" Manuel asks his team, "Let's say we must charge citizens directly for our services and run the precinct as a business. What would we do differently?"

Manuel has found that such conversations almost always result in some worthwhile new ideas. The West Beach culture remains ever vibrant as people keep challenging assumptions and looking at the world differently. This culture breeds a beginner's mind in even the wisest old dogs on the force, and it helps keep team members with different levels of experience working in harmony.

USING A TEAM AGREEMENT TO KEEP EGOS IN CHECK

To promote better balance between ego-driven and group-oriented be-havior, try forging a team agreement that guides people's interactions with one another. These steps will help you formalize "the way we do things around here."

1. **Agree on Norms for Team Interactions**—Gather the en-tire team and ask, "What behaviors do we prefer or require? What behaviors do we prohibit?" Make sure everyone con-tributes to the discussion because you need complete buy-in to the behavioral do's and don'ts. Here are examples of behaviors the team might discuss:

    *   Conflict resolution, such as when it should be escalated to management

    *   Communication guidelines for speaking and listening, such as the need for both patient listening and helpful interruptions

    *   Prohibited behaviors and language that signify bully-ing, belittlement, or disparagement, such as ethnic and gender-based jokes

    *   The best way to express disagreement with a teammate, such as a one-on-one discussion away from the office

    *   Acting with openness, honesty, transparency, ethics, and integrity, even when that means raising issues that make people uncomfortable

    *   Methods for offering feedback and criticism, such as 360 techniques and self-evaluations

2. **Memorialize the Norms in a Team Agreement**—Docu-ment the agreements, and post them where all team mem-bers can see them every day.

3. **Keep the Team Agreement Top-of-Mind**—Review the team agreement when new members join or whenever changing circumstances warrant a revision of "the way we do things around here." Invite the fresh perspectives of new teammates, and make sure veteran teammates share stories that illustrate the team agreement in action.

A team agreement will help all team members, both old and new, maintain their individuality while cooperating with others. I like a term Professor Ron Roberts uses in his book, *The Well-Balanced Leader*. A leader, he proposes, should strive for egolibrium, that perfect balance between other-centric and egocentric behavior.

When the Going Gets Tough

The other day it struck me just how much my emotional state can alter my entire reality. I had sunk into a particularly bad mood after checking my emails and seeing that my collaborator on this book didn't like a section of the most recent chapter I'd sent him (what a jerk), I hadn't heard back from a consulting client who had promised to hire me but kept delaying the final decision (the rat), and I'd heard from my tax accountant that I had grossly underpaid my taxes for last year (the bum). Suddenly I went from a young and confident professional to an abject failure doomed to run out of money in my old age.

My entire world looked as bleak as the dark side of the moon. Thoughts of all the criticism I'd received over the years pushed aside all the praise I'd gotten for my work. Thinking about my career, I could see only all my missteps and all the blind alleys I'd taken, but none of the mountains I'd successfully scaled or any of the peak performances I had achieved. I felt terribly forlorn and guilty and hopeless. How could I write such rubbish? Why would a potential client ever hire such a total loser? Why had I frittered away so much money?

Burdened with this foul mood, I got into my car and drove to the grocery store. The traffic seemed to flow like molasses in January. Other drivers seemed hell-bent on cutting me off or slamming on their brakes or blaring their horns. In the aisles of the grocery store, people kept bumping their carts into mine. One particularly infuriating woman completely blocked the aisle while studying the label of every blasted jar of spaghetti sauce on the shelf. I could hear a little girl wailing for her favorite box of sugary cereal. I just knew that when I finally got to the cash register, an elderly fellow in front of me would take ten minutes looking for an expired credit card. I felt like I was losing my mind!

Then I stopped in my tracks. What's wrong with me? The world hasn't changed. I have. This moment's reality differs not one iota from this morning's reality, when I awoke brimming with energy and enthusiasm for the writing and consulting I was doing. "Jackie, old girl," I said to myself, "you're behaving like the shoemaker who lets her kids go barefoot. Wake up! Screw your head back on straight. "

Right there in the pasta aisle I took some of the advice I give my clients and that I have sprinkled throughout this book. I let myself feel the full brunt of the fear coursing through my body, the hot coal burning in the pit of my stomach, and the deadweight pinning my arms to my side. Then I stopped the gloomy thoughts oozing through my head, focused all my attention on my breathing, took six deep breaths, and recalled the joy I felt riding my bicycle along the Oregon coast with my husband the previous weekend. When I resumed my shopping a few minutes later, I felt as if a fresh breeze had blown all the dark crud from my mind. Goodbye depression! Hello, coherence!

Out of the blue, I saw the perfect creative solution to the problem that my collaborator had pointed out. What a smart man! What a good friend! The new client would call when he was good and ready to hire me. I could wait. If he didn't call, I'd scare up an even better one. My tax accountant? What a lifesaver she was. She did a terrific job looking out for my welfare. I could easily spare the few extra dollars I needed to make Uncle Sam happy. I almost whistled a happy tune as I continued my shopping. The woman ahead of me said hello and pointed out a buy-one-get-one-free offer on Alfredo sauce. A baby girl sitting in her mother's cart tickled my heart with the biggest smile I'd ever seen. What a wonderful world. What a wonderful life.

I know, I know. I'm starting to sound maudlin, but this really did happen. The outward circumstances of my life hadn't changed one tiny bit, but suddenly my experience of life had taken a 180-degree turn from the dark side of the moon to the brightness of a never-setting sun. In the Prologue that opened this book, I spoke of love. Well, the transformation I created for myself that afternoon is exactly the sort of transformation I *love* to bring to teams. Today's complex and often frenetic business world can turn even the most died-in-the-wool optimist into a staunch believer in Murphy's Law. Everything that can go wrong *does* go wrong, and at the worst possible moment. But that's when you stop in your tracks. That's when you listen to your heart. That's when you pick up your bruised confidence, dust it off, and set it back on its feet. That's when you harness the incredible power of optimal emotions.

When the going gets tough, the tough get primal.

NOTES

CHAPTER 1

1. The names of individuals and companies in the stories are fictitious except when referring to a well-known company or person and/or when footnoted.

2. IBM News Release (2010). "IBM Global 2010 CEO Study: Creativity Selected as Most Crucial Factor for Future Success." Extracted from IBM website on February 23, 2012.

3. A. M. Isen, K. A. Daubman, & G. P. Nowicki. (1987). Positive Affect Facilitates Creative Problem Solving. *Journal of Personality and Social Psychology,* 52, 6: 1122–1131.

4. C. K. De Dreu, M. Baas, & B. A. Nijstad. (2008). Hedonic Tone and Activation Level in the Mood–Creativity Link: Toward a Dual Pathway to Creativity Model. *Journal of Personality and Social Psychology*, 94, 5: 739–756.

5. M. Hicks. (2009). Subaru "Love" Isn't Rational. *Washington Times* (June 24).

6. R. McCraty, M. Atkinson, D. Tomasino, & R. T. Bradley. (2006). *The Coherent Heart: Heart–Brain Interactions, Psychophysiological Coherence, and the Emergence of System-Wide Order* (Boulder Creek, CA: HeartMath); D. Childre & B. Cryer, B. (2008). *From Chaos to Coherence: The Power to Change Performance* (Boulder Creek, CA: HeartMath); R. McCraty & D. Childre. (2010). Coherence: Bridging Personal, Social, and Global Health. Alternative Therapies, 16, 4 (July/August).

7. S. David. (2013). How Happy Is Your Organization? *Harvard Business Review* Blog Network.

8. J. Panksepp & L. Biven. (2012). *The Archaeology of Mind: Neuroevolutionary Origins of Human Emotions* (New York: W. W. Norton).

9. D. Goleman, R. Boyatzis, & A. McKee. (2001). Primal Leadership: The Hidden Driver of Great Performance. *Harvard Business Review* (December).

10. S. Shuler & B. D. Sypher. (2000). Seeking Emotional Labor: When Managing the Heart Enhances the Work Experience. *Management Communication Quarterly*, 14: 50.

11. T. D. Wilson, D. T. Gilbert, & B. D. Centerbar. (2003). Making Sense: The Causes of Emotional Evanescence. In I. Brocas & J. D. Carrillo (eds.), *The Psychology of Economic Decisions: Vol. 1. Rationality and Well-Being*, 209–233 (New York: Oxford University Press).

12. R. A. Mccraty, M. Atkinson, & D. Tomasino. (2003). Impact of a Work-place Stress Reduction Program on Blood Pressure and Emotional Health in Hypertensive Employees. *Journal of Alternative and Complementary Medicine*, 9, 3: 355–369; A. W. Bedell & M. Kaszkin-Bettag. (2010). Coherence and Health Care Cost—RCA Actuarial Study: A Cost-Effectiveness Cohort Study. *Alternative Therapies*, 16, 4 (July/August); T. Pipe, V. L. Buchda, S. Launder, B. Hudak, L. Hulvey, K. E. Karns, & D. Pendergast. (2011). Building Personal and Professional Resources of Resilience and Agility in the Healthcare Workplace. *Wiley Online Library* (wileyonlinelibrary.com) (March 13), DOI: 10.1002/smi.1396; B. Barrios-Choplin, R. McCraty, J. Sundram, & M. Atkinson. (1999). *The Effect of Employee Self-Management Training on Personal and Organizational Quality, Institute of HeartMath, Publication* 99-083 (Boulder Creek, CA: HeartMath).

CHAPTER 2

1. J. Panksepp. (2009). Brain Emotional Systems and Qualities of Mental Life. In D. Fosha, D. Siegel, & M. Solomon (eds.), *The Healing Power of Emotion: Affective Neuroscience, Development and Clinical Practice* (New York: W. W. Norton), 19.

2. Panksepp, 4–22.

3. J. Panksepp & L. Biven. (2012). *The Archaeology of Mind: Neuroevolutionary Origins of Human Emotions*, 98–400 (New York: W. W. Norton).

4. W. Isaacson. (2013). *Steve Jobs* (New York: Simon & Schuster), 109.

5. Panksepp & Biven, 352–385.

6. J. Bastable. (2012). *Amazing and Extraordinary Facts: The British at War.* New York: F+W Media.

7. M. Lefevre. (2004). Playing with Sound: The Therapeutic Use of Music in Direct Work with Children. *Child and Family Social Work*, 9: 333–345.

8. B. Bittman, L. Berk, D. Felten, et al. (2001). Composite Effects of Group Drumming Music Therapy on Modulation of Neuroendocrine-Immune Parameters in Normal Subjects. *Alternative Therapies in Health Medicine*, 7, 1: 38–47.

9. Bittman, K. T. Bruhn, C. Stevens, J. Westengard, & P. O. Umbach. (2003). Recreational Music-Making: A Cost-Effective Group Interdisciplinary Strategy for Reducing Burnout and Improving Mood States in Long-Term Care Workers. *Advances in Mind-Body Medicine*, 19, 3/4 (Fall/Winter).

10. P. Tharp, P. (2003). Fortune 500 Tunes into Bang-the-Drum Therapy. *New York Post* (December 5).

11. Mayo Clinic Staff. Stress Relief from Laughter? It's No Joke. Extracted from mayoclinic.com on September 28, 2013.

12. C. Butler. (2011). Laughing May Help Ease Blood Pressure, Boost Mood and Enrich Health in Other Ways. *Washington Post* (October 24).

13. Panksepp & Biven, 368.

14. M. Gladwell. (2002). The Naked Face. *The New Yorker* (August 5).

15. M. Duenwald. (2005). The Physiology of Facial Expressions. *Discover Magazine* (January).

16. E. Jaffe. (2013). The Psychological Study of Smiling. *Association for Psychological Science Observer*, 23: 13–18.

17. S. Stevenson. (2012). There's Magic in Your Smile: How Smiling Affects Your Brain. *Psychology Today*. Published by Ronald E. Riggio, PhD, in *Cutting-Edge Leadership* (June 25).

18. R. E. Kraut & R. E. Johnston. (1979). Social and Emotional Messages of Smiling: An Ethological Approach. *Journal of Personality and Social Psychology*, 37, 9: 1539–1553.

CHAPTER 3

1. J. LeDoux. (1996). *The Emotional Brain: The Mysterious Underpinnings of Emotional Life* (New York: Simon & Schuster), 19, 174–175.

2. LeDoux, 289.

3. J. H. Haidt. (2006). *The Happiness Hypothesis: Finding Modern Truth in Ancient Wisdom* (New York: Basic Books).

4. M. D. Lieberman, N. I. Eisenberger, M. J. Crockett, S. M. Tom, J. H. Pfeifer, & B. M. Way. (2007). Putting Feelings into Words: Affect Labeling Disrupts Amygdala Activity in Response to Affective Stimuli. *Psychological Science*, 18, 5: 421–428.

5. Featured Stories (2013). Extracted from http://www.merck.com/about/featured-stories on October 15, 2013.

6. K. Thomas, Merck Plans to Lay Off Another 8,500 Workers, *The New York Times*, October 1, 2013.

7. LeDoux, 19.

8. D. Rivenburgh. (2013). *The New Corporate Facts of Life: Rethink Your Business to Transform Today's Challenges into Tomorrow's Profits* (New York: AMACOM).

9. S. G. Hofmann. (2008). Cognitive Processes During Fear Acquisition and Extinction in Animals and Humans: Implications for Exposure Therapy of Anxiety Disorders. *Clinical Psychology Review*, 28, 2 (February): 199–210.

10. J. Panksepp. (2009). Brain Emotional Systems and Qualities of Mental Life. In D. Fosha, D. Siegel, & M. Solomon (eds.), *The Healing Power of Emotion: Affective Neuroscience, Development and Clinical Practice* (New York: W. W. Norton), 22.

11. D. Childre & D. Rozman. (2005). *Transforming Stress: The HeartMath Solution for Relieving Worry, Fatigue, and Tension* (Oakland, CA: New Harbinger Publications).

12. D. Childre & B. Cryer. (2008). *From Chaos to Coherence: The Power to Change Performance* (Boulder Creek, CA: HeartMath).

CHAPTER 4

1. D. Goleman & R. Boyatzis. (2008). Social Intelligence and the Biology of Leadership. *Harvard Business Review* (September).

2. G. H. Bower. (1991). Mood Congruity of Social Judgments. In J. P. Forgas (ed.), *Emotion and Social Judgment* (New York: Pergamon), 32–55; J. P. Forgas. (1991). Affect and Social Judgments: An Introductory Review. In J. P. Forgas (ed.), *Emotion and Social Judgments* (New York: Pergamon), 3–30; J. P. Forgas & G. H. Bower. (1987). Mood Effects on Person-Perception Judgments. *Journal of Personality and Social Psychology*, 53: 53–60.

3. R. W. Doherty. (1997). The Emotional Contagion Scale: A Measure of Individual Differences. *Journal of Nonverbal Behavior*, 21: 131–154.

4. L. O. Lundqvist. (1995). Facial EMG Reactions to Facial Expressions: A Case of Facial Emotional Contagion? *Scandinavian Journal of Psychology*, 36: 130–141.

5. S. Colino. (2006). *The Washington Post* Blog (May 30).

6. M. Duenwald. (2005). The Physiology of Facial Expressions. *Discover Magazine* (January 2).

7. Goleman & Boyatzis.

8. Colino.

9. Goleman & Boyatzis.

10. D. Foltz-Gray. (2004). How Contagious Are Your Emotions? O, *The Oprah Magazine* (December): 1.

11. U. Dimberg, M. Thunberg, & K. Elmehed. (2000). Unconscious Facial Reactions to Emotional Facial Expressions. *Psychological Science*, 11: 86–89.

12. D. Goleman, R. Boyatzis, & A. McKee. (2001). Primal Leadership: The Hidden Driver of Great Performance. *Harvard Business Review* (December).

13. R. McCraty. (2003). *The Energetic Heart: Bioelectromagnetic Interactions Within and Between People* (Boulder Creek, CA: HeartMath).

14. Foltz-Gray, 2.

15. McCraty.

16. R. McCraty, R. T. Bradley, & D. Tomasino. (2004–2005). The Resonant Heart. *Shift: At the Frontiers of Consciousness* (December 2004–February 2005).

17. S. Morris. (2010). Achieving Collective Coherence: Group Effects on Heart Rate Variability Coherence and Heart Rate Cynchronization. *Alternative Therapies*, 16, 4 (July/August).

CHAPTER 5

1. B. Yenne. (2012). *Julius Caesar: Lessons in Leadership from the Great Conqueror* (World Generals Series), Kindle Edition (Kindle Locations 885–968) (New York: Palgrave Macmillan).

2. V. Gallese. (2006). Intentional Attunement: A Neurophysiological Perspective on Social Cognition and Its Disruption in Autism. *Brain Research*, 1079, 1: 15–24.

3. R. W. Levenson. (2003). Blood, Sweat, and Fears. *Annals of the New York Academy of Sciences*, 1000, 1: 348–366.

4. V. Gallese.

5. J. Soto, N. Pole, L. Mccarter, & R. W. Levenson. (1998). Knowing Feelings and Feeling Feelings: Are They Connected? Paper presented at the Society for Psychophysiological Research, Denver, CO.

6. Levenson.

7. P. Ekman. (2003). *Emotions Revealed: Recognizing Faces and Feelings to Improve Communication and Emotional Life* (New York: St. Martin's Press); R. Banse & K. R. Scherer. (1996). Acoustic Profiles in Vocal Emotion Expression. *Journal of Personality and Social Psychology*, 70, 3: 614; Mark Coulson. (2004). Attributing Emotion to Static Body Postures: Recognition Accuracy, Confusions, and Viewpoint Dependence. *Journal of Nonverbal Behavior*, 28, 2 (Summer).

8. A. Bechara, H. Damasio,. & A. R. Damasio. (2000). Emotion, Decision Making, and the Orbitofrontal Cortex. *Cerebral Cortex*, 10, 3 (March).

9. A. Bechara. (2004). The Role of Emotion in Decision-Making: Evidence from Neurological Patients with Orbitofrontal Damage. *Brain and Cognition*, 55: 30–40.

10. J. Steinhauer. (2010). John Boehner and the Politics of Crying. *New York Times* (November 6).

11. T. Harnden. (2008). Bill Clinton: Tears Won Hillary New Hampshire. *The Telegraph* (January 9).

12. A. R. Hochschild. (1983). *The Managed Heart: The Commercialization of Human Feeling*. Berkeley: University of California Press.

13. C. Brotheridge & A. Grandey. (2002). Emotional Labor and Burnout: Comparing Two Perspectives on "People Work." *Journal of Vocational Behavior*, 60: 17–39.

14. R. Alsop. (2013). Is It Ever Acceptable to Cry or Shout on the Job? *BBC Capital Blog* (September 12).

15. V. L. Brescoll & E. L. Uhlmann. (2008). Can an Angry Woman Get Ahead? : Status Conferral, Gender, and Expression of Emotion in the Workplace. *Psychological Science*, 19, 3: 268–275. Retrieved from PsychInfo database.

16. C. K. Goman. (2011). Communicating Across Cultures. American Society of Mechanical Engineers (March). Extracted from ASME.org on November 29, 2013.

CHAPTER 6

1. Sony Corporate History. Extracted from www.sony-europe.com on December 11, 2013; J. C. Collins & J. I. Porras. (1994). *Built to Last: Successful Habits of Visionary Companies* (New York: HarperCollins).

2. Mary Helen Immordino-Yang. (2004). TEDx Manhattan Talk; Mary Helen Immordino-Yang. (2011). Musings on the Neurobiological and Evolutionary Origins of Creativity via a Developmental Analysis of One Child's Poetry. *LEARNing Landscapes*, 5, 1 (Autumn).

3. J. LeDoux. (1996). *The Emotional Brain: The Mysterious Underpinnings of Emotional Life* (New York: Simon & Schuster), 19.

4. LeDoux, 289.

5. Brenda Patione. (2013). Desperately Seeking Sensation: Fear, Reward, and the Human Need for Novelty Neuroscience Begins to Shine Light on the Neural Basis of Sensation-Seeking. Extracted from the DANA Foundation on December 27, 2013.

6. Eric Foster. (2004). Research on Gossip: Taxonomy, Methods, and Future Directions. *Review of General Psychology*, 8, 2: 78–99.

7. J. C. Collins & J. I. Porras. (1994). *Built to Last: Successful Habits of Visionary Companies* (New York: HarperCollins).

8. Dan P. McAdams. (2001). The Psychology of Life Stories. *Review of General Psychology*, 5, 2: 100–122.

9. E. Tronick. (2009) Multilevel Meaning Making and Dyadic Expansion of Consciousness Theory. In D. Fosha, D. Siegel, & M. Solomon (eds.), *The Healing Power of Emotion: Affective Neuroscience, Development and Clinical Practice* (New York: W. W. Norton), 88.

CHAPTER 7

1. Debbie Millman. (2010). *How to Think Like a Great Graphic Designer* (New York: Allworth Press).

2. Albert Rothenburg & Carl Hausman. (1976). *The Creativity Question* (Durham, NC: Duke University Press).

3. M. Jung-Beeman, E. M. Bowden, J. Haberman, J. L. Frymiare, S. Arambel-Liu, et al. (2004). Neural Activity When People Solve Verbal Problems with Insight. *Public Library of Science Biology*, 2, 4: e97, DOI:10.1371/journal.pbio.0020097.

4. Rothenburg & Hausman.

5. R. P. Chi & A. W. Snyder. (2011). Facilitate Insight by Non-Invasive Brain Stimulation. *Public Library of Science One*, 6, 2: e16655, DOI:10.1371/journal.pone.0016655.

6. G. Berns. (2010). Iconoclast: *A Neuroscientist Reveals How to Think Differently.* Cambridge, MA: Harvard Business Review Press.

7. A. Cain. (2002). Archimedes, Reading, and the Sustenance of Academic Research Culture in Library Instruction. *Journal of Academic Librarianship*, 28, 3: 115–121.

8. R. A. Dodds, T. B. Ward, & K. G. Smith. (2012). A Review of Experimental Research on Incubation in Problem Solving and Creativity. In M. A. Runco (ed.), *Creativity Research Handbook* (Cresskill, NJ: Hampton Press).

9. Rothenburg & Hausman.

10. Dodds, Ward, & Smith.

11. BBC Documentary. (2013). *Horizon: The Creative Brain How Insight Works.*

12. S. Sandkühler & J. Bhattacharya. (2008) Deconstructing Insight: EEG Correlates of Insightful Problem Solving. *Public Library of Science One*, 3, 1: e1459, DOI:10.1371/journal.pone.0001459.

13. Flora Beeftink, Wendelien van Eerde, & Christel G. Rutte. (2008). The Effect of Interruptions and Breaks on Insight and Impasses: Do You Need a Break Right Now? *Creativity Research Journal* (October).

14. A. M. Hayashi. (2001). When to Trust Your Gut. *Harvard Business Review*, 79, 2: 59–65.

15. L. Robinson. (2012). *Divine Intuition: Your Inner Guide to Purpose, Peace, and Prosperity* (San Francisco: Jossey-Bass); Alan Deutschman. (2004). Inside the Mind of Jeff Bezos. *Fast Company* (August).

16. G. Braden. (2008). *The Spontaneous Healing of Belief: Shattering the Paradigm of False Limits* (New York: Hay House).

17. A. Bechara, H. Damasio, D. Tranel, & A. R. Damasio. (1997). Deciding Advantageously Before Knowing the Advantageous Strategy. *Science*, 275: 1293–1294.

18. R. T. Bradley, R. McCraty, M. Atkinson, & M. Gillin. (2008). Nonlocal Intuition in Entrepreneurs and Non-Entrepreneurs: An Experimental Comparison Using Electrophysiological Measures. Forthcoming In *Regional Frontiers of Entrepreneurial Research* (Boulder Creek, CA: HeartMath).

19. G. Hodgkinson, J. Langan-Fox, & E. Sadler-Smith. (2008). Intuition: A Fundamental Bridging Construct in the Behavioral Sciences. *British Journal of Psychology*, 99: 1–27.

20. Craig Karges. (1999). *Ignite Your Intuition: Improve Your Memory, Make Better Decisions, Be More Creative and Achieve Your Full Potential* (Kansas City, MO: HCI).

21. Hodgkinson, Langan-Fox, & Sadler-Smith.

22. B. Dunn, H. C. Galton, R. Morgan, D. Evans, et al. (2010). Listening to Your Heart: How Interoception Shapes Emotion Experience and Intuitive Decision Making. *Psychological Science*, 21, 12: 1835–1844.

23. Hodgkinson, Langan-Fox, & Sadler-Smith.

24. B. D. Dunn, T. Dalgleish, & . D. Lawrence. (2006). The Somatic Marker Hypothesis: A Critical Evaluation. *Neuroscience and Biobehavioral Reviews*, 30: 239–271.

CHAPTER 8

1. Creating Employee Loyalty & Engagement Through New Hire Orientation with Lara Morrow of Beryl Companies (2011). http://www.beryl.net/content/creating-employee-loyalty-engagement-through-new-hire-orientation.

2. R. F. Baumeister & M. R. Leary. (1995). The Need to Belong: Desire for Interpersonal Attachments as a Fundamental Human Motivation. *Psychological Bulletin*, 117, 3: 497–529.

3. Paul J. Zak. (2012). *The Moral Molecule: How Trust Works* (New York: Penguin, Kindle Edition).

4. J. Bartz, J. Zaki, N. Bolger, & K. N. Ochsner. (2011). Social Effects of Oxytocin in Humans: Context and Person Matter. *Trends in Cognitive Sciences*, 15, 7 (July).

5. R. F. Baumeister & M. R. Leary.

6. K. L. Freiberg. (1987). The Heart and Spirit of Transformational Leadership: A Qualitative Case Study of Herb Kelleher's Passion for Southwest Airlines. *UMI Dissertation Services* (UMI No. 8714632).

7. Irving L. Janis, *Victims of Groupthink* (Boston: Houghton Mifflin, 1972), 9; Irving L. Janis, *Groupthink: Psychological Studies of Policy Decisions and Fiascoes*, 2nd rev. ed. (Boston: Houghton Mifflin, 1983), 16.

8. B. Mullen, T. Anthony, E. Salas, & J. E. Driskell. (1994). Group Cohesiveness and Quality of Decision Making: An Integration of Tests of the Groupthink Hypothesis. *Small Group Research*, 25: 189.

9. Keith Sawyer. (2008). *Group Genius: The Creative Power of Collaboration* (New York: Basic Books).

10. Charlan Nemeth, B. Personnaz, M. Personnaz, & J. A. Goncalo. (2004). The Liberating Role of Conflict in Group Creativity: A Study in Two Countries. *European Journal of Social Psychology*, 34: 365–374.

11. R. W. Boss & M. L. McConkie. (1981). The Destructive Impact of a Positive Team-Building Intervention. *Group and Organization Studies*, 6: 45–56.

12. Extracted from http://www.basf.com/group/corporate/us/en/about-basf/diversity/success-stories and http://www.basf.com/group/corporate/us/en/news-and-media-relations/science-around-us/mosquito-nets-save-lives/story on March 11, 2014.

13. Thomas Lewis, Fari Amini, Fari, & Richard Lannon. (2007). *A General Theory of Love* (Vintage reprint, Knopf Doubleday, Kindle Edition).

14. Brian Uzzi & Jarrett Spiro. (2005). Collaboration and Creativity: The Small World Problem. *American Journal of Sociology*, 111, 2 (September): 447–504.

CHAPTER 9

1. Robert C. Ginnett. (1987). *First Encounters of the Close Kind: The Formation Process of Airline Flight Crews* (Colorado Springs, CO: Department of Behavioral Sciences and Leadership, U.S. Air Force Academy).

2. J. E. Driskell & E. Salas. (1992). Collective Behavior and Team Performance. *Human Factors: The Journal of the Human Factors and Ergonomics Society*, 34: 277.

3. S. Silverman, R. E. Johnson, N. McConnell, & A. Carr. (2012). Arrogance: A Formula for Leadership Failure. *The Industrial-Organizational Psychologist* (July).

4. Extracted from http://www.allmusic.com/album/beethoven-complete-string-quintets-mw0001414930 on March 7, 2014.

5. K. Murayama & A. J. Elliot, (2011). Achievement Motivation and Memory: Achievement Goals Differentially Influence Immediate and Delayed Remember–Know Recognition Memory. *Personality and Social Psychology Bulletin*, 37: 1339–1348.

6. Debbie Millman. (2010). *How to Think Like a Great Graphic Designer* (New York: Allworth Press).

7. J. M. Keynes. (1936) *The General Theory of Employment, Interest and Money* (London: Macmillan).

8. R. P. Chi & A. W. Snyder. (2011). Facilitate Insight by Non-Invasive Brain Stimulation. *Public Library of Science One*, 6, 2: e16655. doi:10.1371/journal.pone.0016655

9. S. H. Carson, J. B. Peterson, & D. M. Higgins. (2003). Decreased Latent Inhibition Is Associated with Increased Creative Achievement in High-Functioning Individuals. *Journal of Personality and Social Psychology*, 85, 3: 499–506.

INDEX